WASHINGTON IN FOCUS

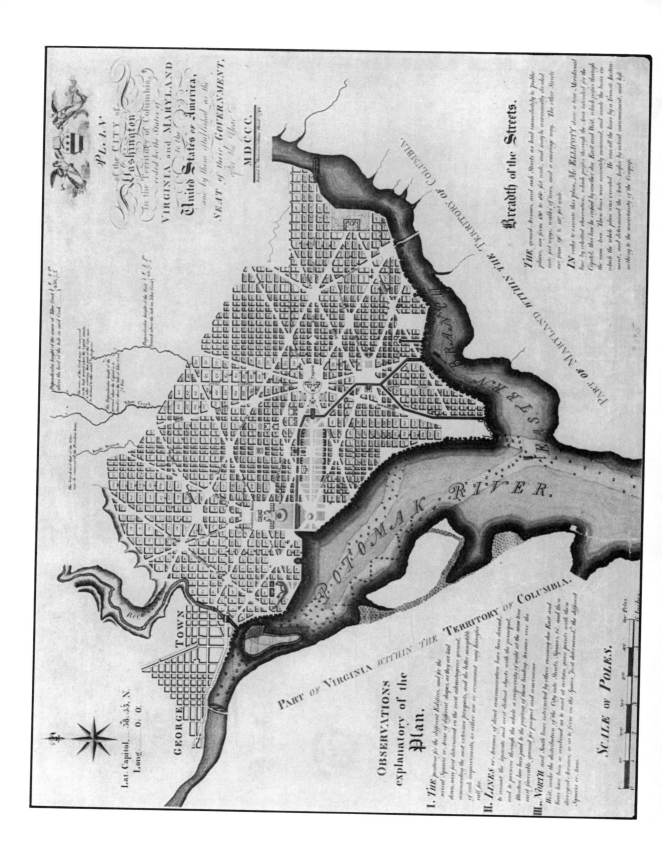

WASHINGTON IN FOCUS

THE PHOTO HISTORY OF THE NATION'S CAPITAL

PHILIP   BIGLER

VANDAMERE PRESS
a division of AB Associates

Published by
Vandamere Press
A Division of AB Associates
P.O. Box 5243
Arlington, Virginia
22205

Copyright 1988 by Vandamere Press

Library of Congress Cataloging-in-Publication Data

Bigler, Philip.
    Washington in focus.

    Bibliography: p.
    Includes index.
    1. Washington (D.C.)--History--Pictorial works.
2. Washington (D.C.)--Description--Views.
3. Washington (D.C.)--History. I. Title.
F195.B54 1988   975.3   88-23096
ISBN 0-918339-07-3

Manufactured in the United States of America. This book is set in Bembo. Typography by Chronicle Type and Design, Washington, D.C. Cover Photograph by Jerry Dreo.

Dedicated to my parents, Charles and Bernice Bigler

Acknowledgements

During the research and preparation of *Washington in Focus*, many people graciously offered their time, advice, and assistance. First, I would like to thank Lew Merletti, the Freedom of Information Officer with the United States Secret Service, for his help in obtaining the photographs of the Roosevelt Bunker. Elsa Santoyo at the Executive Office Building, likewise provided many excellent pictures and was a wealth of information concerning the history of the building. At Congressional Cemetery, Cindy Warren kindly gave me access to her historical files and Diana Kaiser and Catherine Milarczic at the Hotel Washington were similarly helpful.

The Presidential Library system was an outstanding source of both information and photographs. In particular, I would like to thank Jim Cedrone at the John Kennedy Library and Carol Briley at the Harry S Truman Library for their assistance. I would also like to acknowledge Mark Renovitch (Roosevelt Library), E. Philip Scott (Johnson Library), and Richard Holzhausen (Ford Library).

The United States Armed Services have enthusiastically supported this project. I especially would like to recognize Russell Egnor with the Department of the Navy and Sgt. Joseph Steele with the United States Marine Corp Band for their help. At the Mount Vernon Ladies' Association, Ann Rauscher was similarly kind.

I am indebted to Leroy and Eva Belle Mimms and to James Lancaster for sharing with me their memories of Washington. Likewise, I would like to express my thanks to Jo Ann Keller for obtaining her father's recollections of his days with the Washington Senators. At the National Park Service, Philip Walsh has once again been a crucial source of information and contacts while Bill Clarke has graciously loaned me several of his personal photographs.

Art Brown, my publisher at Vandamere Press, has provided the needed direction and advice for this book. Pat Berger, my editor, has likewise enhanced the quality of the text through her extensive grammatical knowledge while Jerry Dreo has again provided an outstanding photograph for the cover. Linda Bigler, my beloved wife, has similarly devoted many hours to proof-reading and has been a source of constant encouragement.

Finally, I would like to thank some very special friends and exceptional people who worked diligently on the index and the final proof-reading: Tom and Carole Mulhearn, Jeff Dunson, Bridget Bonham, Philip and Wende Walsh, and Karen Bierman. Without these people, this book could never have been finished.

Table of Contents

CHAPTER ONE
"Washington City [is] Not a City At All"

In April 1789, George Washington was inaugurated as the nation's first President under procedures established by the recently ratified United States Constitution. New York City was then serving as the provisional capital of the United States while Congress initiated an investigation to determine a more suitable site for a permanent seat of government. Most delegates favored moving the capital to an existing city in the North but such proposals were resisted by Southern legislators. In 1790, as debate raged and the issue remained unresolved, the entire federal government was temporarily relocated to Philadelphia.

The following year, Secretary of the Treasury Alexander Hamilton introduced a detailed and far-reaching fiscal program that required all of the 13 states to submit their Revolutionary War debts to the federal government for final payment. Ostensibly, the plan was designed to create a national debt while ensuring complete funding of old war bonds. Hamilton's scheme was also carefully calculated to establish the principle of supremacy of the federal government. Most Southerners, including Thomas Jefferson and James Madison, bitterly opposed the program, arguing that the proposed law unjustly favored the Northern states which continued to carry large debts while their Southern counterparts had successfully retired the bulk of their loans. Furthermore, thousands of unscrupulous speculators had already successfully purchased old war bonds at deflated prices from their original owners to redeem them at substantial profits later, once the federal legislation was adopted. Since Southern support was vital for the success of Hamilton's financial program, the Secretary agreed to a compromise. In return for Southern support for the passage of the legislation, the new proposed federal capital would be located permanently in the South.

Shortly after adoption of Hamilton's legislation, Congress authorized President Washington to survey potential sites for the federal capital along the Potomac River. He finally chose a location just south of the tobacco port of George Town, conveniently situated near his Mount Vernon estate. Although the region consisted primarily of undeveloped marshland, it was strategically positioned along the navigable portion of the Potomac River with easy access to the lucrative markets of the west and its rich resources. Furthermore, the area was sufficiently removed from the Atlantic Ocean and was thereby protected from marauding foreign navies.

Both Virginia and Maryland readily agreed to cede tracts of land for the creation of a 10-mile-square federal district. Pierre L'Enfant was then commissioned by Congress to design an entirely new city, a capital carved from the wilderness which would reflect the infant nation's republican ideals. An architecture in the classical revival style reminiscent of ancient Greece and Rome was adopted for most government buildings while wide boulevards and avenues were designed to link symbolically the various branches of government. The Capitol building was intended to be the city's focal point, majestically positioned on the summit of Jenkin's Hill, the District's highest point.

Congress mandated the completion of the city's major buildings by 1800. Final surveying and construction commenced almost immediately with the cornerstone of the President's House set in 1792 followed by that of the Capitol. Simultaneously, private entrepreneurs, sensing business opportunity, built a tavern and a brewery nearby to service the needs of the federal government.

In early 1800, Washington's successor, John Adams, visited the new federal district and wrote: "I like the Seat of Government very well and shall sleep, or lie wake next winter in the President's house." The process of relocating the government from Philadelphia began that summer. Although the entire federal bureaucracy consisted of only 136 employees, the task of moving voluminous records, legal documents, and furniture required several weeks. Finally, on November 17, the entire Congress formally convened in joint session in the north wing of the uncompleted Capitol building. The new capital had at last begun to function.

The city, however, by all standards was still remote and primitive. First Lady Abigail Adams became hopelessly lost in Maryland while en route to join her husband in Washington. Later, after arrival, she lamented, "Washington City was not a city at all." Albert Gallatin, a member of Congress, confirmed Mrs. Adams' account writing, "Our location is far from being pleasant or even convenient. Around the Capitol are seven or eight boarding houses, one tailor, one shoemaker, one printer, a washing-woman, a grocery shop, a pamphlets and stationery shop, a small dry goods shop, and an oyster house. This makes the whole of the Federal City as connected with the Capitol. At the distance of three-fourths of a mile, on or near the Eastern Branch, lie scattered the habitations of Mr. Law, of Mr. Carroll, the principal proprietors of the ground, half a dozen houses, a very large but perfectly empty warehouse, and a wharf graced by not a single vessel. And this makes the whole intended commercial part of the city."

When coupled with the region's disagreeable summer climate the District's remote location conspired to keep the resident population small. When the government officially began its operation in 1800, only 8,144 people lived in the city with 24 percent of these in regions still classified as rural. During the ensuing years, the resident population of Washington gradually grew. By 1860, however, on the eve of the Civil War, the city remained a small, provincial town, dwarfed by New York, Philadelphia, Boston, and the other great metropolises of the North.

In addition to Washington's hot and humid climate, the area's naturally swampy conditions contributed to the misery of District residents in the summer. The nation's third President, Thomas Jefferson, pledged: "Grumble who will, I will never pass those two months [July and August] on tidewater," and he regularly abandoned Washington for the cool foothills of Virginia. Similarly, Aleksandr Borisovich Lakier, a Russian aristocrat who visited the United States in 1859, observed, "[in the summer] the streets and hotels were virtually empty, the heat had driven the diplomatic corps to the seashore, and it is no exaggeration to say that the city . . . resembled a desert."

Despite such obstacles during the early years of the Republic, new government buildings were being erected constantly. The Capitol, the White House, the Treasury, the Patent Office, and the Navy Yard became the city's most notable landmarks; but the city still lacked symmetry and order. As Lakier reported: "In Washington, itself, one can find architectural work of all styles, beginning with the most ancient and ending with an absolutely newly invented and unprecedented one. It is worth taking a look at the Smithsonian Institution and then at the Treasury Department across from it: the former is a true likeness of a medieval Norman Castle, and one simply does not know why it has appeared on the bank of the Potomac, quite inappropriately for a building designated for the spreading of enlightenment. Meanwhile, the Treasury Department is modeled on the Greek temple of Minerva in Athens, as are a large number of federal buildings in Washington." The renowned English novelist, Charles Dickens, observed in 1842 that, "[Washington consists of] spacious avenues that begin in nothing and lead nowhere, streets a mile long that only want houses, roads, and inhabitants; public buildings that need but a public to be complete." Lakier agreed stating that the city, "looks like a big village whose wide streets were built Lord knows for whom or what . . . Even the Capitol abandoned at the end of town, towers in deathly silence . . . while the home of the president . . . barely visible behind the trees, a two-story house sufficient for a private family and not at all conforming to the expectations of a European."

The Plumbe Daguerreotype

Until 1840, knowledge of early Washington was limited to the recorded written observations made by visitors and inhabitants. Unfortunately, these accounts rarely took note of the commonplace, relegating such mundane matters to the less interesting and less important aspects of everyday life. Even the artists and illustrators of the period frequently idealized Washington's setting, liberally moving or inaccurately positioning buildings to fit their needs. They too ignored the less aesthetic aspects of city life and thereby rendered only a facsimile of reality.

In 1840, however, a pioneering photographer, John Plumbe, opened the National Daguerrian Gallery and Photographic Depot on Pennsylvania Avenue. The daguerreotype, a process which produced on specially treated copper plates ". . . the most minute details of a scene . . . with an exactitude and sharpness well-nigh incredible," had been perfected just a year earlier. For the first time, an unadulterated historical record could be produced, one that captured a setting as it existed for a brief moment in time.

During the winter of 1846, Plumbe announced an ambitious project to photograph the capital's major government buildings. He produced five quality daguerreotypes for his *Capital Views*, including the Capitol, the White House, and the Patent Office. Shortly thereafter, however, Plumbe abandoned his Washington and East Coast business ventures and travelled west where he became involved in a monumental scheme to build a southern transcontinental railroad, a project which ended in his financial ruin. Finally, in despair and destitute, Plumbe committed suicide. All traces of his early photographic work simply disappeared.

In 1972, a collector of photographic memorabilia, Michael Kessler, purchased several aged and discolored daguerreotypes at a California flea market. After the material was carefully cleaned, the copper plates were sent to the Library of Congress for study. Experts excitedly confirmed that the photographs were Plumbe's five *Capital Views* and the Library purchased the material in 1977.

With the discovery of the Plumbe daguerreotypes, the beginning of the archive of photographic history of the nation's capital had been found. Each later photographer would now follow in the legacy of this little known man.

The Port of George Town

The settlement of the upper tidewater regions of the Potomac River basin did not begin until the mid-18th century. Prior to that time, early settlers in Virginia and Maryland preferred the fertile lands of the lower Chesapeake Bay area which provided easy access for ocean-going vessels involved in the international tobacco trade. As the soil became depleted and the plantations of the lower James and Rappahannock Rivers became less productive, ambitious settlers began to migrate north.

Unlike the great James River plantations, the farms of Maryland and northern Virginia were modest operations, relatively small and removed from navigable waterways. These "middling planters" were forced to diversify, growing wheat and corn along with the revenue-producing tobacco. Still, the English mercantile system required the shipment of such colonial staples abroad, thus necessitating a centralized system of storage. The ports of Alexandria and George Town were created to meet these needs as places where local farmers could send their crops to await shipment. The ports also had the distinct advantage of shortening the turnaround time for the ocean-going vessels which were vulnerable to a native naval worm which bored holes through the wooden hulls of ships while in Virginia waters.

George Town and its rival port, Alexandria, both thrived during the colonial period. As the gateway to the west, George Town served as a staging area during the French and Indian War (1754-1761). From there General Edward Braddock's troops marched out toward Fort Duquesne (Pittsburgh) where they launched a doomed attack against the French garrison.

After the American Revolution, the end of the mercantile system helped George Town in con-

Library of Congress

The Foxhall-Columbia Foundry served as a major supplier of cannons and mortors to the nation's military. Nearby is the Georgetown University observatory. Georgetown was the first Catholic college in the United States, founded by Bishop John Carroll in 1792.

Library of Congress

The Port of George Town just prior to the Civil War. The area served as the southern terminus for the C&O Canal as well as an important commercial center.

tinuing to thrive. It became an important business area for the region complete with numerous taverns, warehouses, mills, and other enterprises. When Congress decided to create a federal district for the new capital, the port became a meeting place for commissioners and contractors working in the city; however, it lacked many of the amenities typical of the larger, more cosmopolitan cities to the north. Abigail Adams called George Town, "the very dirtyest Hole I ever saw for a place of any trade or respectability of inhabitants. It is only one mile from me but a quagmire after every rain." George Town's fortunes peaked in the 19th century with the completion of the Chesapeake and Ohio Canal. The venture promised cheap water transportation inland but was doomed by the simultaneous development of the railroad. As the canal's southern terminus, however, the port continued to operate and maintained a degree of independence from the city of Washington. By 1871, the encroachment of the federal city made the two areas indistinguishable and the town was incorporated into Washington, forever losing its official separate identity.

The C&O Canal

After the American Revolution, George Washington returned to his Mount Vernon estate to attend to domestic matters. He soon developed an active interest in the possibility of constructing a canal north of George Town to allow the navigation of the Potomac River beyond Great Falls. Such a waterway was expected to contribute to the development of the port of George Town while providing coveted access to the lucrative western territories.

In 1785, the Patowmack Company was chartered to begin construction of the canal. Washington, who was selected as the company's president, assisted in the initial surveys for the canal. Because of the expense involved in the construction of the locks and their relative vulnerability to damage from ice and debris, members of the Patowmack Company decided instead to build a series of bypass canals wherever practical. These were little more than man-made channels that allowed river

traffic to avoid the Potomac's dangerous falls and rapids. At Great Falls, however, the river's dramatic 76-foot drop necessitated the construction of a series of five locks, an engineering feat that required over two decades to complete. Finally by 1800, flat bottom boats from western areas were routinely able to use the river and its canals to carry supplies of flour, corn, whiskey, and furs to market in the east. However, the impossibility of returning upstream led most boatmen to abandon their 75-foot barges in George Town, selling them for lumber, and returning to their homes on foot.

Floods, bad weather, and erosion hindered the early canal's operation, ordinarily allowing navigation of the Potomac for a mere two-month period during the summer. Meanwhile, a group of adventurous businessmen, encouraged by the success of the Erie Canal in New York, began forming plans to expand the original canal to link

Library of Congress

Barge traffic on the C&O Canal, circa 1900. The lateral waterway eventually spanned 185.7 miles. High maintenance cost and the development of the railroad led to its decline.

A view of the canal looking toward George Town, circa 1860. The canal was prone to flooding from the Potomac River and portions of it were routinely closed for repairs.

Washington with the distant Ohio River. The Chesapeake and Ohio (C&O) Company, was created to undertake the project which planned for the construction of an entirely new, lateral waterway adjacent to the Potomac.

On July 4, 1828, ground-breaking ceremonies were held near Little Falls, some five miles north of George Town with President John Quincy Adams as the featured guest. At the same time but unknown to the group at Little Falls, similar ceremonies were being conducted in Baltimore to mark the beginning of construction on the Baltimore & Ohio Railroad, the transportation wonder which would ultimately bankrupt the C&O and virtually all other canal operations.

From 1828 through 1850, workers and engineers labored on the C&O canal, opening each small section immediately upon completion. When finally finished, the six-foot deep, 60-foot wide waterway spanned an incredible 185.7 miles, including 74 locks and seven dams. A six-foot wide towpath had been built simultaneously for the horses which would power the barges along the canal.

Water transportation on the C&O was slow but relatively cheap, costing roughly half that of overland transport. The canal's period of greatest success occurred during the 1870s when more than 500 barges operated on the C&O canal, most carrying massive amounts of coal to the east. The upkeep on such an extensive and elaborate transportation system was enormous, however, especially since the Potomac River habitually flooded the canal, necessitating costly repairs to locks, aqueducts, and dams. Despite such obstacles, the C&O operated until 1924 when a catastrophic flood over its entire length made repair financially unrealistic and forced the waterway to close to all commercial operations.

For the next several years, the remains of the canal were allowed to deteriorate further. Local residents frequently vandalized the waterway, breaching its walls to free the stagnant water which harbored thousands of mosquitos and emitted a powerful stench. In 1938, recognizing the canal's historical significance, the federal government purchased the waterway. The following year, the National Park Service declared it as a national landmark and began efforts to restore it to its 19th-century grandeur. Today, the C&O Canal is a source of numerous recreational activities.

The Aqueduct Bridge

The completion of the C&O canal was seen as a potential economic disaster for the port of Alexandria, Virginia. Since George Town was the southern terminus of the canal, all inland shipping and traffic would be off-loaded at the rival port, effectively bypassing Alexandria located several miles further downstream. In desperation, Virginia residents created the Alexandria Canal Company with a mandate to build a seven-mile extension canal along the west bank of the Potomac River. The Aqueduct Bridge was designed and planned to connect this canal with the C&O canal on the opposite bank of the river. The span would allow canal barges to cross over the Potomac River and proceed south to Alexandria.

The construction of the bridge started in 1833, took over a decade to finish, and cost a staggering $575,000. Upon completion, the Aqueduct Bridge was 1,456 feet long and rose 40 feet above the Potomac. It consisted of eight piers and two stone abutments. Like most canal systems, maintenance of the bridge proved costly and the vital pumps which kept water flowing through the bridge's troughs frequently failed. Similarly, the financial difficulties of the C&O canal reduced the bridge to being an impressive engineering feat and an expensive anachronism.

During the Civil War, the federal government temporarily assumed ownership of the bridge and its channel was drained of water. In May 1861, several thousand troops of the Army of the Potomac used the Aqueduct Bridge to cross into Virginia where they seized the Arlington plantation of Robert E. Lee and the neighboring city of Alexandria. The bridge continued to operate as an important Potomac crossing throughout the war.

After the Civil War, the span was returned to private ownership. The trough was again filled with water and barge traffic was able once more to use the bridge. To increase revenues, however, a toll road was built on top of the span but excessively high rates discouraged traffic and failed to

Library of Congre[ss]

The Meigs Aqueduct piped water to the District of Columbia. The Aqueduct Bridge is also visible in the background, May 12, 1859.

The Aqueduct Bridge with Georgetown University in the background. The Bridge was designed to carry barge traffic from the C&O Canal across the Potomac River to the connecting Alexandria Canal. During the Civil War, however, the bridge's trough was drained of water to allow passage of Union troops into Confederate Virginia.

generate the desired money. When Congress threatened to build a public bridge just north of George Town in 1881, the owners agreed to sell the bridge to the federal government to avoid bankruptcy.

Under federal ownership, the bridge still required constant maintenance and repair. In 1916, it was decided to replace the bridge with a new, modern span. Named for Francis Scott Key, the new bridge connected George Town with Rosslyn, Virginia, and was complete with trolley tracks. The Key Bridge, made from reinforced concrete, opened in January 1923. By then, the Aqueduct Bridge became completely useless and, as part of a project during the Depression, the span was demolished in 1933. The unsightly piers stood forlornly in the Potomac River until 1962 when they were removed as part of a beautification project.

The Smithsonian Institution

James Smithson, an English scientist best known for his work in chemistry and mineralogy, died in 1829 without an heir while residing in Genoa, Italy. The enigmatic scientist mysteriously bequeathed his extensive fortune to the United States government, stipulating in his will that the funds be used to, "found at Washington, under the name of the Smithsonian Institution, an establishment for the increase and diffusion of knowledge among men." Despite Smithson's obvious generosity, Congress was initially reluctant to accept the $500,000 inheritance. Representatives questioned the legality of the federal government's administering a private estate but, finally, after years of disagreement and debate, the legislature finally agreed to charter the Smithsonian Institution on August 10, 1846. Congress, however, issued the charter with the mandate that the institution should function both as a museum and a research facility.

The following year, architect James Renwick was retained to design the principal Smithsonian building. Renwick incorporated several architectural styles adapted from the Near East and created a multitowered, red stone building which became informally known as *The Castle*. Although the building was architecturally impressive, it met with severe criticism from area residents including John Hay, the first Secretary of the Smithsonian, who felt the building was too costly and ostentatious. Other critics faulted *The Castle*'s dras-

tic departure from Washington's traditional classical revival style. In 1851, the American sculptor, Horatio Greenough, denounced the facility writing that, ". . . the dark form of the Smithsonian palace rose between me and the white Capitol . . . Tower and battlement, and all that medieval confusion, stamped itself on the halls of Congress, as ink on paper! Dark on that whiteness—complication on that simplicity." Yet despite these objections, *The Castle* building remained for decades the chief architectural landmark on the Mall between the Capitol and the Washington Monument.

The Castle building originally housed the Smithsonian's entire collection of natural history specimens along with its laboratory and research facilities. In 1904, the remains of the museum's founder, James Smithson, were brought from Europe and solemnly reinterred to a special crypt near the building's central entrance.

Over the ensuing years, the Smithsonian Institution has gradually expanded, adding new buildings while simultaneously dispersing its ever increasing research facilities and collections. Currently, the Castle serves only as the administrative center of the Smithsonian complex which encompasses an impressive array of 16 museums and galleries. Over 20 million people visit the Washington area museums annually to view the Institute's impressive collections and exhibits.

The Castle building of the Smithsonian Institution. James Renwick designed the new museum building but its Gothic design was widely criticized in Washington for its dramatic departure from the capital's traditional classical revival style.

Congressional Cemetery

In the early 19th century, Washington was a remote and often inaccessible city. Members of Congress frequently were forced to travel for weeks over poor roads and primitive waterways to attend sessions of the legislature. Once in the capital, the malarial climate and unbearable summer heat caused many of their deaths. In 1812, Congress was forced to purchase 100 plots at the Washington Parish Burial Grounds for the interment of members who died while in residence in the District of Columbia. Because of government interest in the Washington Burial Grounds, its name was formally changed to Congressional Cemetery and, despite continued private ownership, it is unofficially considered to be the first national cemetery.

Fourteen senators and over 60 representatives were eventually buried at Congressional Cemetery even though most politicians continued to prefer interment in their native states. Congress, however, continued to appropriate funds to erect cenotaphs at Congressional Cemetery for any legislator who died while in office, despite burial elsewhere. From 1838 through 1877, dozens of identical, unsightly monuments were commissioned until the practice was finally suspended.

Since death was a frequent but unpredictable reality in the 19th century, many prominent individuals were allowed temporary repose in the Public Vault at Congressional Cemetery while more elaborate funeral services were finalized. Three American presidents—William Henry Harrison, John Quincy Adams, and Zachary Taylor—were briefly interred at the cemetery before their remains were transported back to their respective states. Likewise, former First Lady Dolley Madison was buried at Congressional Cemetery for over eight years until friends finally made arrangements for returning her body to Montpelier, Virginia.

The most notable of the early interments at Congressional Cemetery was Elbridge Gerry, one of the 56 signers of the Declaration of Independence. In 1813, Gerry was elected to serve as Vice President. Unlike his predecessors, he took an active interest in presiding over the United States Senate. In November 1814, while en route to a legislative session, Gerry collapsed and died. After his interment, Congressional colleagues authorized a prominent memorial to honor Gerry in recognition of his role as one of the nation's founding fathers.

During the Civil War, many of the Union soldiers who died in Washington's numerous military hospitals were buried at area cemeteries including Congressional. In June 1864, a group of women were employed at the Washington Arsenal preparing rifle cartridges for Union troops when a hot fuse ignited a large amount of loose black powder in the building. The resulting explosion killed 21 of the women and the terrible aftermath was graphically reported by *The Evening Star*, ". . . the charred remains of those who had perished were laid upon the ground and covered over with canvas." President Lincoln and over 2,000 mourners attended the funeral services at Congressional Cemetery where 14 of the women were buried in a common grave with a single memorial erected to mark the site.

The following year, on April 14, 1865, Louis Paine attempted to kill Secretary of State William Seward as part of John Wilkes Booth's plan to murder President Lincoln and other high government officials. Fearing imminent arrest, Paine quickly took refuge on the grounds of Congressional Cemetery. As Louis Weichmann recounted later in a book concerning the assassination, "Paine discovered a marble vault which had been built above the ground. He lifted off the slab with his back, and then crept inside, replacing the stone. In this gloomy abode, the companion of worms and dirt, he remained three days and nights, without shelter or sufficient clothing to protect him from the cold." Paine was later apprehended after he left the cemetery's grounds and was hung in July 1865 along with three other conspirators. Four years later, in one of the last acts of his presidency, Andrew Johnson allowed family

Library of Congress

Cenotaphs at Congressional Cemetery. Congress authorized such monuments through 1877 for any Representative or Senator who died while residing in the District of Columbia despite actual interment elsewhere. Congressional Cemetery, located in southeast Washington, is the final burial place for such notables as Mathew Brady, John Philip Sousa, J. Edgar Hoover, and Elbridge Gerry.

members to claim the bodies of those who had been executed. The remains of Davey Herold, the young 19-year-old accomplice who had accompanied Booth during his two week exodus through southern Maryland, were removed to Congressional Cemetery where they were privately interred next to the graves of his two deceased sisters. The grave, however, is still unmarked because of the heinous nature of his crime.

Since the 19th century, Congressional Cemetery has been expanded to 32 acres. It continues to be an active cemetery, averaging slightly over 50 burials per year. Other notable burials include Mathew Brady, the prominent Civil War photographer; William P. Wood, first director of the United States Secret Service; John Philip Sousa, the "March King"; and J. Edgar Hoover, the director of the FBI.

The Capitol

Of all the government buildings in Washington, the United States Capitol was considered the most important during the early 19th century. The original founding fathers firmly believed that the Congress would be the most representative branch of the government and the one closest to the people. It would be the very bastion of American democracy. Thus, with great ceremony and pride, President George Washington solemnly set the cornerstone of the building on September 18, 1793.

The Senate wing was the first portion of the Capitol completed. On November 22, 1800, all of the nation's 32 senators and 106 representatives met in joint session there to hear an address by President John Adams. The separate, detached House of Representatives building was not completed until the following year but structural defects led its members to denounce the facility as *the Oven*. Poor acoustics also necessitated the installation of thick, heavy red draperies to muffle echoes.

Work on a central colonnade to connect the two legislative houses was interrupted by hostilities with the British in 1812. Two years later, Congress was forced to evacuate Washington hastily after the rout of American militiamen at Bladensburg left the city defenseless. British troops quickly captured and occupied the Capitol. The enemy soldiers delighted in ransacking and looting the building before finally setting it on fire. The Capitol was virtually destroyed and led a French newspaper to decry, "How could a nation eminently civilized, conduct itself at Washington with as much barbarity as the old banditti of Attila? . . . Is not this act of atrocious vengeance a crime against all humanity?" With a return to peace in 1814, Architect Benjamin Latrobe began the difficult task of reconstructing the Capitol, but he was replaced in 1817 by Charles Bulfinch. Bulfinch added a copper-sheathed dome and a central colonnade complete with 24 Corinthian sandstone columns to the Capitol. This formed an impressive portico on the east facade. To replace the books destroyed by the British during the looting of the Capitol, Thomas Jefferson donated over 6,000 volumes from his personal library to the government. His collection, described by Francis C. Gray as ". . . without a question the most valuable in the world," was used to form the nucleus of the Library of Congress which was located in the Capitol.

The continued westward expansion of the nation and the subsequent addition of new states severely cramped the Congress and strained the Capitol's facilities. In 1850, the legislature appropriated $100,000 for a much needed expansion. The Bulfinch dome was to be replaced by a larger and even more impressive, steel-tiered dome and two new, larger wings were to be added for the House and Senate.

The first portion of the project was completed in 1857 when the House chamber opened. Aleksandr Lakier, a Russian visitor to Washington, attended a meeting of the House shortly thereafter and reported: "Everyone wears a black frock-coat or tails and sits where he pleases. Had I not felt regret for the nice new furniture and carpet in the House of Representatives, I would not even have

Library of Congress

The earliest known photograph of the House chamber, 1861. Here angry debates raged between Congressmen concerning slavery and Southern rights.

The United States Capitol in 1860. The dome remained unfinished at the time of the outbreak of the Civil War. The old Washington City Canal was located on the Mall but was no longer in use and had virtually become an open sewer.

noticed the rude, but perhaps comfortable, position of the feet raised by a son of the plains above the head of his neighbor, and the nasty habit many Americans have of chewing tobacco." The debates concerning slavery dominated sessions of Congress during this period and frequently erupted into open bitterness and hostility. Indeed, in 1856, after delivering a two-day tirade against slavery in the Senate, Charles Sumner was severely cane-whipped in the chamber by a Southern representative, prompting several members to begin wearing sidearms to the Capitol. By 1861, seven Southern states had withdrawn from the Union. President Abraham Lincoln's inauguration was held on the east portico under the shadow of civil war with the unfinished Capitol dome, sheathed in scaffolding and surrounded by cranes, as a backdrop to the joyless ceremony. Despite the impending hostilities, Lincoln ordered work on the Capitol to continue ". . . as a sign we intend the Union shall go on." During the war, the Capitol was protected by several gun batteries scattered around the 120-acre grounds. Likewise, fed-

eral troops were barracked in the building at various times. After the nearby battles of Second Manassas and Antietam, wounded from the front were hospitalized and cared for in the building. Lincoln's pledge to finish the Capitol was finally fulfilled on December 2, 1863 when the 19-foot statue, *Freedom*, was affixed to the top of the dome. A 35-gun salute to the nation was fired to mark the occasion. Just 16 months later after his assassination, the President became the first American to lie in state in the new Rotunda, an honor that has since been extended to only 24 other Americans.

The Capitol has undergone several reconstructions since its completion. The most extensive one occurred during the late 1950s when the east portico was dismantled and expanded. During that time, the original 34-foot Bulfinch columns, unable to bear the increased weight of the heavier structure, were removed. The columns were then carelessly stored at the Poplar Point Nursery in southwest Washington, neglected and forgotten until they were transferred to the National Arboretum.

Lincoln's First Inauguration

The 1860 presidential election was bitterly contested among four rival candidates. Abraham Lincoln received a bare electoral majority but received only 40 percent of the popular vote, exclusively from Northern and Western states. Indeed, the President–elect had failed to capture a single vote in nine Southern states where Lincoln had been inaccurately branded as an abolitionist. The deep South refused to accept Lincoln's election. South Carolina soon seceded from the Union and was joined shortly thereafter by six other cotton-producing states. Together, the rebellious states formed the Confederate States of America and selected Jefferson Davis as the first president of the new country.

Lincoln was deeply distressed by the events surrounding his election and attempted to reassure concerned citizens by visiting several cities en route to Washington for the inaugural ceremonies. After delivering a Washington Day address at Philadelphia's Independence Hall, however, the President–elect was informed of a possible assassination plot in Baltimore and convinced to alter his schedule. Reluctantly, Lincoln secretly travelled through the hostile Maryland city and arrived unannounced in the nation's capital early on the morning of February 23, 1861. Immediately, Southern newspapers lampooned Lincoln, chiding him for covertly entering the city ". . . as a thief in the night." Others contemptuously charged Lincoln with disguising himself as a woman to avoid detection.

Lincoln and his family were provided quarters at the famed Willard Hotel. There, he met regularly with well-wishers but Washington, a Southern town by tradition and inclination, was devoid of the enthusiasm associated with such gala events. Indeed, throughout the District, rumors freely circulated that Lincoln would be denied inauguration and there was open discussion of the possibility of assassination.

Military advisors undertook unprecedented security arrangements to ensure a peaceful transference of power. The inaugural platform, specially constructed on the east steps of the Capitol, was carefully searched for explosives and an armed guard was stationed nearby to deny unauthorized access. Skilled sharpshooters were deployed along the inaugural route down Pennsylvania Avenue and within the Capitol building itself to discourage potential troublemakers. Likewise, on the morning of March 4, two columns of cavalry were dispatched to surround and escort Lincoln's carriage through the streets to the Capitol.

At precisely 12 o'clock, noon, Chief Justice of the Supreme Court Roger Taney, the architect of the insidious Dred Scott decision which had inflamed sectional rivalries in 1857, administered the oath of office to Abraham Lincoln. The new President of a deeply divided United States stepped forward to deliver his first inaugural address. He began: "Apprehension seems to exist among the people of the Southern States, that by the occasion of a Republican administration, their property and their peace and personal security are to be endangered. There has never been any reasonable cause for such apprehension." He went on to appeal to the South to preserve the Union but ominously warned, "In your hands, my dissatisfied fellow-countrymen, and not in mine is the momentous issue of civil war. We are not enemies, but friends. We must not be enemies. Though passion may have strained, it must not break our bonds of affection!" The eloquence of Lincoln's address left most unmoved. Less than six weeks later, Confederate artillery bombarded the federal garrison at Fort Sumter, South Carolina. The Civil War, the most bitter and divisive conflict in American history, had begun. It was a titanic struggle destined to transform the nation's capital forever.

Abraham Lincoln's First Inauguration, March 4, 1861. Seven Southern states had already seceded and armed sharpshooters had been deployed around the Capitol to discourage trouble. Lincoln warned the Confederate states, "In your hands, my dissatisfied fellow-countrymen . . . is the momentous issue of civil war."

CHAPTER TWO
The Union Forever

Washington was still indisputably a Southern town in 1861. Most area residents were openly hostile to the inauguration of the prairie lawyer from Illinois, Abraham Lincoln. As if to attest to that fact, a large Confederate flag, defiantly waving above the Marshall House Hotel in neighboring Alexandria, was clearly visible across the Potomac River.

The Union capital itself was in serious jeopardy that spring since the District's location between two slaveholding states, Virginia and Maryland, threatened to isolate the city. Communications with the pro-Union Northern states could also be disrupted at any time. Furthermore, Washington was virtually defenseless, guarded only by the meager remnants of Washington's ill-trained and poorly equipped home guard comprised mainly of veterans from the War of 1812. This force was hardly a military threat to any invading Confederate army. Still, the elderly Union soldiers diligently guarded the city's three major bridges which spanned the Potomac River into rebellious Virginia. They vowed to resist any Confederate thrust against Washington.

The arrival in April 1861 of the first regular Union troops under the command of the Massachusetts General and politician Benjamin Franklin Butler alleviated the immediate danger. The troops clad in Union blue received a mixed reception; they were warmly welcomed by members of the government but met with icy silence from many of the city's 61,000 citizens. Unquestionably, most of the Union soldiers were disappointed with Washington. They saw that the great government buildings which majestically mimicked ancient Roman and Greek temples were enveloped by a ramshackle town of unpainted buildings and unpaved roads. Furthermore, Washington residents still owned more than 3,000 slaves, a fact that confronted the soldiers from the free states with the specter of the South's system of bondage and left little doubt about the city's sympathies.

The Capitol building itself, the very heart of the federal government and Washington's most notable landmark, remained unfinished with its new dome a mere skeleton of an architect's vision. Similarly, the Washington Monument, begun amidst celebration and ceremony a decade earlier, was not even half-completed. Its grounds were used to corral beef cattle to feed the gargantuan needs of the ever-growing army. A slaughterhouse operated nearby, contributing to the stench which seemed to permeate Washington's air. The old Washington City canal which cut through the central portion of the city remained unused, an open scar on the landscape and a convenient receptacle for trash and sewage.

The Civil War, the nation's most divisive conflict, was destined to change the nation's capital forever. During the ensuing four years of bloodshed from 1861 to 1865, the city served as the center of the war effort. Thousands of unscrupulous speculators and contractors converged upon the city, each anxious to make a fortune from the needs of the army. During this time another man arrived in Washington, an individual whose vision and ingenuity would transform him into the country's foremost photographer and Washington's most prolific chronicler—Mathew Brady.

Mathew Brady

Mathew Brady initially studied photography under Samuel Morse, the inventor of an electronic language for the telegraph. Morse was also credited with bringing L.J.M. Daguerre's photographic process to the United States and establishing the first known school of photography in 1840.

After completing his studies, Brady set up his own studio and aggressively began to seek out prospective clients. The enterprising young photographer soon embarked upon an ambitious project to photograph the nation's leading citizens. Over the next several years, Brady successfully made portraits of such notables as Brigham Young, Thomas Hart Benton, and Edgar Allen Poe along with the great orators of Congress, Henry Clay, Daniel Webster, and John Calhoun. In an effort to complete the project in 1845, Brady traveled to Hermitage, Kentucky to make a daguerreotype of the aged and dying former President, Andrew Jackson. Brady ultimately photographed all American presidents from John Quincy Adams through William McKinley with the exception of William Henry Harrison who died suddenly in 1841 before Brady was practicing his craft.

After years of work, Brady finally published a collection of his portraits entitled, *Brady's Gallery of Illustrious Americans*, in 1850. It included 24 daguerreotypes, each copied individually and reproduced for every volume. The book sold for $20, a staggering sum in those days. It proved to be a noble venture but a financial failure.

Brady and other photographers quickly learned that the daguerreotype process had many limitations, despite its revolutionary technology. Since the photos appeared directly on the exposed copper plates, there were no negatives and production was limited to a single copy. Reproducing the picture required an entire new photograph of the original daguerreotype, a timely and expensive procedure. Likewise, a daguerreotype initially produced a reversed image which could be corrected only by copying the original exposure. Brady and other photographers investigated alternatives to the daguerreotype and quickly adopted the new wet-plate photographic process shortly after its introduction in 1852. The new technique required treating a photographic plate with a noxious solution of collodion, a volatile mixture of sulfuric and nitric acids. Once done, the wet-plate had to be immediately exposed from 5 to 60 seconds and developed, all within a 10-minute time frame. The resulting glass negative, however, could be used indefinitely to reproduce the original photograph on specially treated albumen paper.

Wet-plate photography made photographs readily affordable to the general population and led to the popularity of photographic visiting cards or *cartes de visites* (CDV). The 2-1/2 x 4-inch calling cards were made with special four-lensed cameras which simultaneously produced multiple images on a single plate. The pictures were then mounted on cardboard and sold for a mere 25 cents each or $3.00 per dozen. Photographic studios freely reproduced CDV images of famous and notable personages and sold them to the general public, making the collection of such cards a favorite pastime. Indeed, most American households had special albums to hold and display such cards.

In 1858, Brady expanded his prospering photographic operations to Washington, D.C., opening a new studio at 627 Pennsylvania Avenue on the corner of 7th Street. Alexander Gardner, his able assistant, was placed in charge while Brady returned to his New York firm. As war between the states became inevitable, Brady once again returned to Washington and took up residence in the National Hotel in order to supervise his business. On February 23, 1861, President-elect Abraham Lincoln visited Brady's Pennsylvania Avenue studio to sit for his first official portrait.

The forthcoming Civil War provided enormous business opportunities for the nation's 3,000 photographers. Indeed, over one million soldiers eventually served in the Union army, all eager to have their portraits made in their new, resplendent uniforms.

In July 1861, as the Army of the Potomac left Washington for Bull Run, Brady accompanied the federal troops to the Virginia battlefield, carrying his photographic equipment and supplies in a portable darkroom wagon. For the next four years as forces of the North and South repeatedly engaged in colossal combat, Brady followed the raging armies taking thousands of photographs of wartime fortifications, soldiers, and battlefields. In his efforts to chronicle the story of the Civil War, Brady and his assistants came under hostile fire at both Fredericksburg and Petersburg.

After Lee's surrender in 1865, Brady attempted to exhibit a portion of his massive Civil War collection in Washington. General Grant and others praised Brady's work as an unsurpassed record of the nation's bloodiest conflict, but the public was disinterested. The enormous expenses he had incurred in producing his wartime photographs coupled with ever-increasing competition led to his subsequent financial difficulties. By 1869, Brady could no longer even pay the expense of storing his collection of 8,000 glass negatives. Fearing default and potential foreclosure, Brady urgently petitioned the United States Senate on February 23, 1869, to purchase his collection of Civil War photos:

". . . It is too precious to remain in the hands of any private citizen, and your Memorialist hereby respectfully proposes to dispose of the entire Collection of Views and Portraits, properly mounted, together with the NEGATIVES (as per schedule hereunto annexed,) to CONGRESS, that the same may be placed on permanent exhibition at the National Capitol where the pictures and negatives may be secure from injury or loss by fire; and at the same time, accessible to the historical student, the artist, and the public."

Brady's appeal concluded with an exhaustive catalog of the negatives he wished to sell to the government. The Senate Library Committee agreed only to ". . . inquire into the expediency of securing for preservation by the government, the collection of war views and incidents," but no legislative action was forthcoming.

Two years later, the federal government appropriated such funds to pay only Brady's creditors and took possession of his collection without any financial compensation to the photographer. The action infuriated two former Union generals, Benjamin F. Butler and James Garfield, who were then serving in the House of Representatives. Both demanded that appropriate payment be made to Brady with Garfield contending, "Here is a man who has given 25 years of his life . . . to one great purpose—to preserving national monuments so far as photographic art can do so . . . This man went so far as to send his organization into the field and some of his men were wounded in going near the battlefield to take pictures of the fight that was going on." In 1875, a rider was attached to a sundry appropriations bill which provided $25,000 to Brady for his 6,001 negatives. However, in 1897 when a catalog of the material was finally prepared, it was revealed that careless handling and improper storage of Brady's negatives by the federal government had damaged or destroyed some of the material, reducing the Brady collection to its current size of 5,712 photographs.

Unfortunately, the Congressional action did little to alleviate Brady's financial difficulties. In April 1895, while in Washington, Brady was seriously injured when he was struck by a horse carriage on the corner of 14th Street and New York Avenue. Although he partially recovered from the accident, Brady's health declined and he was hospitalized in the fall. He died on January 15, 1896, in a New York City charity hospital.

Brady's body was returned to Washington, the scene of his most notable work, and he was buried at Congressional Cemetery. A simple granite marker was erected, inscribed ironically with the wrong year of death. Today, as the cemetery's fortunes have declined, Brady's small tombstone is frequently obscured by weeds. It sits forlornly amid the rubble of desecrated monuments and vandalized grave markers. Few people visit Brady's grave but his photographs continue to testify to his achievements. They remain his greatest legacy, a pictorial record of the nation and its capital during its greatest crisis.

Slavery

In a speech delivered before Congress in 1816, John Randolph angrily scolded his fellow slave-holders, "You call this the land of liberty, and every day that passes things are done in it at which the despotisms of Europe would be horror-struck and disgusted." Indeed, the presence of slavery in the nation's capital had become an international embarrassment. Northern representatives were universally infuriated when involuntarily confronted by the realities of the South's so-called *peculiar institution*. Still, because of its location sandwiched between the tobacco producing slave states of Maryland and Virginia, the District of Columbia inevitably served as a convenient and profitable depot for merchants trading in slaves. The *National Intelligencer*, the capital's primary newspaper, regularly ran advertisements from transient slave dealers who completed their transactions in taverns and used the city's jails to hold their cargo.

The slave population of the District peaked in 1830 when the census revealed that over 6,000 slaves were living in the city; most were employed as domestics and house servants. However, by 1860, the number of area slaves had dramatically declined and the freed black population of Washington increased correspondingly.

Petitions to abolish slavery in the federal city were first introduced in Congress in 1814 but, as with most other efforts to regulate slavery, these were opposed by Southern delegations. In 1849, the junior Congressman from Illinois, Abraham Lincoln, cosponsored legislation that encouraged the voluntary manumission of slaves in the District while appropriating ample federal funds to compensate the city's slave owners. The measure was rejected, but in the following year, Senator Henry Clay succeeded in passing the Compromise of 1850 which ". . . prohibit[ed] within the District the slave trade." Slave ownership, however, remained unchallenged. The Congressional law did little to regulate the supply of slaves coming to Washington since slave dealers in Alexandria, Virginia, continued to sell to the city's residents.

During the Civil War, President Lincoln ordered the abolition of slavery in the capital in 1862 in the District of Columbia Emancipation Act. In a message to Congress, he justified his actions in writing, "I have never doubted the constitutional authority of Congress to abolish slavery in this District; and I have ever desired to see the national capital freed from the institution in some satisfactory way." Encouraged by the success of the law, the proscription against slavery was later codified in the 13th Amendment to the Constitution.

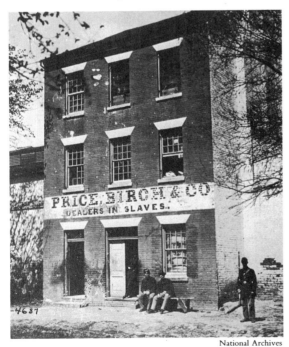

National Archives

The Price, Birch and Company slave pens in Alexandria, Virginia, 1863. The slave trade was abolished in the District in 1850 but slave ownership was permitted until 1862.

Slaves were often confined to cells before auction. In Washington, most of the city's 3,000 slaves worked as domestics.

Union Troops in Washington

Shortly after Confederate forces shelled the federal garrison at Fort Sumter, South Carolina, in April 1861, President Abraham Lincoln issued an urgent appeal for military volunteers to quell the rebellion and restore the Union. The capital was particularly vulnerable to a potential Confederate attack since neighboring Virginia had recently joined the ever-growing number of rebellious states. Likewise, riots in Baltimore, the nation's third largest city, threatened to disrupt vital communication links with the Northern states, thereby completely isolating the District.

Since no one had anticipated the need to protect Washington from invasion by its adjacent states, no forts or other defenses had yet been constructed in the area. Thus, a dramatic Southern assault in the spring could easily overpower the city's meager militia force comprised primarily of aged War of 1812 veterans and end the Civil War by capturing the Union capital. Aware of the imminent danger to the nation, Brigadier General Benjamin Franklin Butler, the colorful but haughty commander of the 8th Massachusetts Infantry, answered Lincoln's request for troops and arrived in Washington with three regiments. This arrival fortified the city and greatly reduced the immediate danger of attack.

In the ensuing weeks, thousands of Union reinforcements continued to arrive in Washington. Soldiers from the 69th New York were forced to bivouac on the grounds of Georgetown University while troops from Colonel Ambrose Burnside's 1st Rhode Island Regiment were quartered in the Patent Office. Other soldiers were housed in the Capitol and allowed to wander freely throughout the building and frequently pilfered Congressional stationery and other souvenirs.

Over 200,000 soldiers were eventually stationed in the immediate vicinity of Washington. Most were deployed in the numerous defensive forts then being rapidly constructed around the perimeter of the city while others were stationed

National Archive

The 96th Pennsylvania Infantry Regiment during drill at Camp Northumberland. Union troops arrived in Washington in April, 1861, to defend the capital from Confederate attack. Many were housed in government office buildings during the initial stages of the war.

The 9th Veteran Reserve Corps at Camp Fry in April 1865. Many of the Union soldiers in Washington were stationed in the 68 defensive forts which completely surrounded the city.

near the three crucial bridges that spanned the Potomac River into Confederate Virginia. Still, duty in Washington was usually remote from the fighting and frequently became tedious and routine. Troops often sought relief from boredom by playing cards, gambling, and drinking. Brawls involving soldiers became so common in Washington's numerous taverns that the War Department imposed a strict 9:30 PM curfew on enlisted troops stationed in the area. Still, Corporal Charles Moulton recounted that ". . . persons are arrested every day on charges preferred for selling liquor to soldiers, which is strictly against the law." During the war, Washington's notorious red light area thrived and was eventually inhabited by over 4,000 prostitutes. A newspaper reporter wrote, "[The capital] was the most pestiferous hole since the days of Sodom and Gomorrah. The majority of the women on the streets were openly disreputable . . . in fine, every possible form of human vice and crime, dregs, offscourings and scum had flowed into the capitol [sic] and made of it a national catch-basin of indescribable foulness."

General Joe Hooker attempted to confine the city's brothels to a small area just southeast of the Treasury Department. This effort proved to be only modestly successful but led soldiers and residents to scornfully refer to the prostitutes as *hookers*.

Throughout the military camps in Washington, disease posed a major problem. Indeed, an estimated three-fourths of all Civil War deaths were caused by various camp illnesses, including typhus, scurvy, tuberculosis, smallpox, and typhoid. Contaminated water supplies and poor sanitation likewise were responsible for over 45,000 deaths from dysentery. Washington's 21 military hospitals were constantly overcrowded with desperately ill soldiers. On May 11, 1864, William Christman, a young soldier from Pennsylvania, died at Lincoln Hospital in southeast Washington. The private's remains were taken across the Potomac River and buried on a remote section of the antebellum estate of Robert E. Lee. His burial was the first in what would eventually become the nation's most honored burial ground, Arlington National Cemetery.

Washington Fortifications

In May 1861, a substantial force of 10,000 Union soldiers rapidly crossed the Potomac River into Virginia and occupied the neighboring port city of Alexandria. Simultaneously, additional federal forces were dispatched to seize the Arlington plantation of Colonel Robert E. Lee. In an effort to discourage a Confederate counteroffensive, two defensive forts were erected on Lee's estate. The forts were eventually supplemented by 66 other fortifications which completely encircled Washington and effectively blocked all major avenues of access leading into the city.

Washington's defensive perimeter proved to be a formidable obstacle. During the peak years of the Civil War, the forts were routinely manned by over 50,000 Union soldiers and deployed 762 artillery pieces and 74 mortars. Most of the fortifications boasted 20-foot thick, earthen walls which were impervious to enemy artillery fire. The sur-

rounding moats combined with felled trees made infantry assault suicidal. Likewise, two seacoast fortifications armed with potent 15-inch smoothbore Rodman guns commanded the Potomac's southern approaches.

By 1864, General Ulysses S. Grant had successfully forced the war southward toward the Confederate capital of Richmond. Seemingly remote from any danger, many of Washington's forts fell into disrepair and were allowed to deteriorate. The vigilance of the troops lessened correspondingly. By summer, Lee's dwindling Confederate army was cornered at Petersburg, Virginia, compelling their commander into an untenable defensive position. In a desperate effort to break the siege, Lee ordered General Jubal Early to launch a daring surprise attack against Washington, anticipating that such a northern thrust would compel Grant to abandon his advantageous position in or-

National Archives

The sally port at Fort Stevens, 1861. The only battle in the District of Columbia was fought here in 1864 when General Jubal Early attempted to attack Washington. President Lincoln watched the battle and was the only American Chief Executive to actually come under enemy fire while in office.

The 15-inch Rodman gun at Battery Rodgers in Alexandria, Virginia. Such weapons discouraged the Confederates from attempting to launch a naval attack against Washington up the Potomac River.

der to protect the Union capital.

On July 11, 1864, after an arduous summer march, Early's army converged upon Fort Stevens which commanded the northern approaches into the city. Confronted by the imposing fortress and deterred by its 17 cannons, Early paused to rest and regroup his exhausted troops and delayed his attack until the following day. Ironically, Fort Stevens was uncharacteristically vulnerable to a siege; it was defended by a mere 1,500 men, mostly convalescent soldiers commandeered from the city's hospital wards. The delay in the attack proved disastrous since it allowed Major General Alexander McCook to hastily reinforce the garrison with seasoned veterans of the Army of the Potomac's renowned VI Corps.

News of the impending battle spread rapidly throughout Washington and attracted hundreds of spectators, including President Lincoln, to Fort Stevens to watch the confrontation. During Early's futile attack, the President came under hostile fire and consented to withdrawing from the front only upon the urgent pleas of Captain Oliver Wendell Holmes. The Confederate assault on the Union garrison failed to breech the fort's walls and Early's troops were forced to withdraw in defeat, losing the only battle fought in the District of Columbia. Grant's powerful army continued to press Lee at Petersburg and eventually forced the surrender of the entire Confederate army.

At the conclusion of the war in 1865, Washington's forts immediately became obsolete and were abandoned, left to decay and deteriorate. Only Fort Whipple, located on Lee's antebellum estate, remained operational and was eventually renamed Fort Myer, the headquarters of the 3d United States Infantry, *the Old Guard*. Forts Stevens, Marcy, and Ward were eventually restored and are now operated as historic sites.

The Washington Arsenal

The Anacostia River flows into the Potomac River just below Greenleaf Point, the southernmost site in the District of Columbia. When drafting the original designs for the federal capital, Pierre L'Enfant quickly recognized the area's strategic value and favored constructing a defensive fortress on the peninsula to protect the city from potential invasion. By 1794, a modest gun battery on the site commanded the Potomac River approach to Washington while plans for a more formable fortification were being devised.

In 1803, work finally began on the Washington Arsenal, replacing the obsolete gun emplacement at Greenleaf Point. The new garrison initially served as a centralized distribution depot for weapons and ordnance. The fortress, however, was completely destroyed in 1814 when the American army burned the facility to prevent its capture by the British army during the War of 1812. After the war, the arsenal was rebuilt and enlarged to include a new federal penitentiary. The prison, designed by the architect of the Capitol, Charles Bulfinch, could incarcerate up to 160 inmates. It remained in operation until 1862.

During the Civil War, the District's proximity to Confederate Virginia and the rebel army placed increased demands on the Washington Arsenal. It quickly became the Union's largest and most im-

Library of Congress

The Washington Penitentiary was located at the Washington Arsenal. The Lincoln conspirators were tried and executed here in 1865. The unfinished Washington Monument is visible in the distance.

The Washington Arsenal was a major distribution point for ordinance and weapons. Here several Wiard guns await transport to Union troops, May 1862.

portant supply depot. Throughout the war, artillery pieces, caissons, and munitions were carefully stockpiled on the grounds while dozens of civilian employees continually assembled rifle cartridges for the troops. Likewise, battle-damaged cannon were repaired and restored there.

The Washington Arsenal's location along the banks of the Potomac River made it an ideal site for field testing new weapons developed by countless inventors and contractors who hoped to patent and sell them to the Union army. Each device was carefully test-fired and evaluated but inferior workmanship and poor casting methods often made the program extremely hazardous. Still, President Lincoln took an active and ongoing interest in the program. He visited the arsenal regularly to observe testing of the weapons, including such novelties as 121-barrel artillery rifles, repeating guns, and breech-loading muskets.

After the President's assassination in 1865, the individuals charged with the murder were imprisoned within the old penitentiary on the arsenal's grounds. Each prisoner was confined in complete isolation, their heads shrouded and their legs chained. The trial was held before a nine member military tribunal which heard the evidence and testimony in a specially prepared courtroom within the prison compound. All the defendants were found guilty; four of them, including the boarding house owner, Mary Surratt, were sentenced to death. A gallows was erected within the prison walls and on July 7, 1865, the conspirators were executed before a large gathering of Union soldiers. Their remains were quickly buried without ceremony in unmarked graves nearby.

The arsenal's importance radically declined with the return to peace and the disbanding of the Union army. The penitentiary was demolished in 1867 and the bodies of the conspirators were returned to the families shortly thereafter for private interment. Several other Civil War-era storehouses located nearby were also razed while others were allowed to fall into disrepair. In 1901, Secretary of War Elihu Root, succeeded in establishing the Army War College at the arsenal and the fort once again began to prosper. In 1948, it was renamed in honor of General Lesley J. McNair who lost his life during the Normandy invasion in World War II. Today, the military installation serves as the headquarters for the Military District of Washington.

The Old Brick Capitol

On August 24, 1814, a large contingent of British regulars landed just south of Washington near Benedict, Maryland. After routing an undisciplined force of American militia, the British paraded triumphantly through the now undefended capital. Although still primitive by European standards, Washington was nonetheless a significant military objective and the British soldiers quickly began ransacking, looting, and burning federal buildings, including the newly completed Capitol and President's House.

Shortly thereafter the British abandoned the ravaged city in order to continue their campaign up the Chesapeake while a disheartened United States Congress returned to the ruins and desolation. Many legislators renewed old arguments that the capital's Potomac site was unsuitable as a seat of government and demanded that the city of Washington be abandoned for a safer and more hospitable location in the north. Residents of the

Library of Congress

The execution of Captain Henrich Wirz, C.S.A. Wirz was the commandant of the notorious Andersonville Prison Camp, where over 13,000 Union prisoners died from malnutrition, exposure, and disease.

District of Columbia, fearing that such a move would lead to financial ruin, quickly acted to thwart any such relocation. Local merchants and citizens collected funds for construction of a temporary brick capitol to house the legislature while the original structure could be rebuilt. Located on First Street, the Brick Capitol was completed in late 1815 and the Congress formally convened there in December. Two years later, James Monroe was sworn in as the nation's fifth president during ceremonies conducted on the front steps of the building, thereby establishing the continued tradition of outdoor inaugural ceremonies.

Congress returned to the more spacious chambers of the reconstructed Capitol in 1819 and the Brick Capitol was returned to private ownership. The structure was converted into a boarding house which primarily served members of Congress during their stay in Washington. Senator John Calhoun of South Carolina, the renowned spokesman for states rights and a former Vice-President, was its most prominent resident until his death in 1850.

During the decade immediately preceding the American Civil War, the Old Capitol building was allowed to deteriorate, inhabited only by vagrants and destitutes. But with the onset of hostilities in 1861, the federal government once again assumed ownership of the building. The windows were boarded up and sealed while the structure's various apartments were converted into prison cells to incarcerate Confederate spies, rebel sympathizers, Southern soldiers, and local undesirables. Belle Boyd, a crafty Southern agent who successfully extorted military intelligence from federal officials and supplied the crucial information to Confederate commanders, was imprisoned in the Old Capitol Prison as were many other female Southern sympathizers. Corporal Charles Moulton who served briefly as a guard at the prison, wrote, "In regard to the female prisoners...if they don't obey orders, we are strictly upheld in shooting them as quick as anybody else. One of our corps did fire at one of these fair dam-

The Old Brick Capitol was transformed into a prison during the Civil War. The windows were boarded up and the rooms were converted into cells. Belle Boyd, a Confederate spy, was incarcerated here along with many other rebel sympathizers.

sels one day last week and came very near to hitting her. They have got the idea into their heads that they can do just as they please and are very impertinent."

Perhaps the most notorious of the prisoners was Captain Henry Wirz, C.S.A. During the war, Wirz served as commandant of the Andersonville prison camp in Georgia and had supervised the incarceration of over 39,000 Union prisoners. Over 13,000 of his prisoners died from various maladies including malnutrition, dysentery, consumption, and exposure, prompting Judge Advocate General Joseph Holt to charge that "[Wirz] was destroying more Union soldiers than rebel generals were butchering on the battle-

field." The inhuman treatment of federal soldiers at Andersonville led to Wirz's conviction as a war criminal by a military tribunal. On November 10, 1865, he was executed on the grounds of the Old Brick Capitol before a large gathering of Union soldiers, some of whom perched on nearby trees for a better view of the hanging.

With the conclusion of the Civil War, the need for the prison ceased and the building once again fell into disrepair and disuse. In the late 1920s, Chief Justice of the Supreme Court William Howard Taft convinced Congress to demolish the building for the construction of a new Supreme Court Building which now stands on the site.

Lincoln's Second Inauguration

Amidst the political and social upheaval caused by the American Civil War, a presidential campaign was waged in 1864. Abraham Lincoln was nominated for re-election and was joined on the Union ticket by a "War" Democrat from Tennessee, Andrew Johnson. They were opposed by the popular former commander of the Army of the Potomac, George C. McClellan. The outcome of the election, however, was decided on the battlefield when General William Tecumseh Sherman captured and burned Atlanta and marched to the sea with his forces, thereby dooming the Confederacy and ensuring Lincoln's re-election.

On March 4, 1865, a large crowd gathered in Washington on the east lawn of the Capitol for Lincoln's second inauguration. Despite the cold, damp weather, most were optimistic and the

Library of Congress

The crowd at the Capitol awaiting the Inaugural Parade, March 4, 1865. The boarding houses in the background were primarily occupied by Congressmen while in residence in the District. They were demolished in 1872.

mood was festive for Grant's powerful armies were readying to launch a final offensive against Lee's beleaguered forces, entrenched at Petersburg, Virginia. However, the solemnity of the ceremonies was disrupted when the Vice President-elect arrived at the Capitol drunk. Allegedly Johnson, weakened by a viral infection, had attempted to fortify himself against the blustery weather with two stiff drinks of whiskey and had become unintentionally inebriated. He embarrassed himself during the swearing-in ceremonies when he suddenly grasped the Bible and mumbled, "I kiss this Book in the face of my nation of the United States." Likewise, during his scheduled address to Congress and the President, Johnson rambled and was often incoherent in his remarks.

Despite Johnson's incoherence, Lincoln was formally escorted outside to the east front of the Capitol where Chief Justice of the Supreme Court Salmon Chase administered the oath of office precisely at 12 noon. Lincoln then stepped forward to a small iron table which had been specially constructed for the occasion from scraps of the newly completed Capitol dome and began to deliver his address. After four brutal years of bloodshed, the end of the nation's most divisive war was finally in sight and Lincoln used the event to urge reconciliation with the South. His brief but eloquent remarks concluded, "With malice toward none; with charity for all; with firmness in the right, as God gives us to see the right, let us strive on to finish the work we are in; to bind up the nation's wounds; to care for him who shall have borne the battle, and for his widow, and his orphan—to do all which may achieve and cherish a just and lasting peace among ourselves, and with all nations." While Lincoln was delivering his address, Alexander Gardner, a former associate of photographer Mathew Brady, was making several exposures of the historic occasion. Years later after careful analysis of the photographs, it was revealed that John Wilkes Booth was in attendance at the ceremonies. Indeed, the actor who would kill Lincoln just

Abraham Lincoln delivering his Second Inaugural Address. John Wilkes Booth and his fellow conspirators attended the ceremonies at the Capitol. They would successfully assassinate the President just six weeks later.

six weeks later had received priority admission to the ceremonies through a romantic interest, the daughter of Senator Hale of New Hampshire. Perched on the platform just above Lincoln, Booth would later record in his diary, "What an excellent chance I had to kill the President if I had wished on inauguration day." Gardner's photographs further revealed the presence of Booth's accomplices. Directly below Lincoln during the address were Lewis Paine, John Surratt, Davey Herold, and George Atzerodt, all of whom would later be charged in the murder of the President and three of them hanged. After the ceremonies ended and the crowd slowly dispersed, few anticipated that the greatest tragedy of the Civil War was still before them.

Ford's Theater

The First Baptist Church on 10th Street in northwest Washington was leased in 1861 to an enterprising theater owner, John Ford, who transformed the building into the city's foremost playhouse. Originally known as Ford's Atheneum, the theater was tragically destroyed by fire shortly after its opening but was quickly rebuilt, improved, and enlarged to accommodate crowds of up to 1,700 patrons.

During the Civil War, President Abraham Lincoln regularly attended performances at Ford's, generally preferring the plays of William Shakespeare but enjoying light drama as well. Shortly before he travelled to Pennsylvania to deliver the Gettysburg Address, the President watched the production of *The Marble Heart* which featured the well-known actor, John Wilkes Booth.

John Wilkes Booth, originally from nearby Bel Air, Maryland, appeared regularly on the Washington stage despite his fanatical support of slavery and Southern secession. As the South gradually succumbed to the powerful Union armies, Booth devised a diabolic scheme to rescue the Confederacy. His plan was to abduct President

Library of Congress

The Surratt Boarding House. John Wilkes Booth and his conspirators plotted here initially to kidnap President Lincoln. The owner, Mary Surratt, was executed for her association with Booth.

Lincoln and ransom him only upon the release of thousands of captured Confederate soldiers then being held in Northern prison camps. Booth recruited several accomplices to aid in the plot, including John Surratt, an active Confederate courier, who freely offered the use of his mother's H Street boarding house as a headquarters for the conspiracy.

On April 6, 1865, General Lee finally accepted the inevitable and surrendered his depleted Confederate forces at Appomatox Court House. In Washington, virtually the entire city erupted in celebration at news of the surrender of the Army of Northern Virginia. Corporal Charles Moulton recounted, "Everybody was feeling joyous . . . all the public and private buildings were decked with the colors and numerous appropriate mottoes, and bands of music were playing patriotic airs all over the City. But the grandest display was in the evening. Almost every building was illuminated and fireworks were displayed throughout the City. The Capitol presented a gorgeous scene, it being lit up from cellar to the extreme top of the dome, looking like a massive sheet of fire. All of the department buildings were also extensively illuminated, every widow pane having a candle in it, the outside walls being literally robed with flags and transparencies of all sorts." John Wilkes Booth, however, was despondent over the military outcome of the Civil War and remained determined to avenge the South. Informed of the President's plans to attend the final performance of Laura Keene in *Our American Cousin* at Ford's Theater on April 14, Booth hastily began final preparations to assassinate the President and murder other key government officials.

Ford's Theater planned a gala welcome for the President to celebrate the Union's glorious and hard-fought victory over the South. A special song, *Honor to Our Soldiers*, had been composed and inserted at the end of the play while the traditional Presidential box was elaborately festooned with flags and featured a framed portrait of George Washington.

When the President and his theater party arrived at Ford's, they were escorted to the box by John Parker, a bodyguard assigned to protect Lincoln that evening. After Lincoln was safely seated and the play had resumed Parker inexplicably abandoned his post, leaving the President completely undefended. Shortly after 10 PM, Booth entered the Presidential box and fatally shot Lincoln. Booth then escaped by leaping down to the stage and, despite breaking his leg, successfully fled out a back door and mounted his awaiting horse.

National Archives

Ford's Theater on E Street. President Abraham Lincoln was fatally wounded here on April 14, 1865 by John Wilkes Booth.

When army surgeons finally reached the wounded President, they pronounced the wound mortal but were successful in restoring a faint pulse. Several soldiers were quickly commandeered to carry Lincoln's body across the street to the Petersen boarding house where he died the following morning without ever regaining consciousness.

In the aftermath of the assassination, panic reigned throughout the city. A. McCree, a young soldier from Iowa City, recounted, "The city is full of excitement this evening, people running wild . . . the streets you may say is full of guards and it is not safe for a country boy to be out far from home." John Ford, the owner of the theater, was quickly arrested and incarcerated briefly in the Old Capitol Prison. The theater was seized and, despite Ford's expressed desire to reopen, was confiscated by federal authorities. The building was turned over to the Quartermaster Corps which gutted the interior and converted it into office space. Later, the old theater briefly served as the Army Medical Museum and finally as a proc-

essing depot for pension requests. In 1893, a tragic accident occurred when the third floor of the theater collapsed, killing 22 men and forcing the closing of the building.

In 1938, some 68 years after Lincoln's assassination, ownership of the building was ceded to the National Park Service. Once again, it was converted into a museum, a repository for historian Osborn Oldroyd's collection of Lincoln memorabilia. In 1968, after extensive architectural and historical research, the building was reconstructed and restored to its original 1865 appearance. Once again it became an active stage while the basement area was reserved for Lincoln artifacts and assassination relics including the derringer pistol Booth used to kill the President. Surratt's boarding house on H Street where the conspirators frequently met remains in private ownership. Today in the heart of Washington's Chinatown, the H Street residence operates as a small grocery store.

The Victory Parade

President Lincoln's untimely assassination in April, 1865, brought an abrupt end to the joy and excitement in Washington surrounding the surrender of Lee's Army of Northern Virginia. The nightly illuminations and the innumerable galas quickly ended, replaced by black mourning crepe and memorial tributes in honor of the martyred Chief Executive.

While the nation grieved, the final acts in the drama of the Civil War were being played out. Confederate General Joe E. Johnston finally capitulated, surrendering the last major rebel army. Likewise, President Jefferson Davis was captured and arrested in Georgia. In Washington, the trial of the eight conspirators charged in the Lincoln assassination began at the Arsenal compound as

The Victory Parade of the Grand Army of the Republic, May 1865. For two days, the battle-hardened veterans marched down Pennsylvania Avenue in a final display of military pageantry.

Library of Congress

The Presidential Reviewing Stands. President Andrew Johnson, Secretary of War Edwin Stanton, and other government leaders watch as Union troops parade.

the victim, Abraham Lincoln, was being laid to final rest in Springfield, Illinois. A decent interval had passed and government leaders decided to grant the victorious Union armies a triumphal parade through the streets of the capital before being formally disbanded.

Four reviewing stands were erected on the White House and Treasury Department lawns for the President and other official dignitaries. Each was elaborately decorated with Union battle flags, streamers, and flowers. On May 23, President Andrew Johnson, Secretary of War Edwin Stanton, and Lieutenant General U.S. Grant gathered to watch the procession. Promptly at 9 A.M. a signal gun was fired to mark the beginning of the parade. General George Gordon Meade headed the procession followed closely by Generals Sheridan and Custer and 10,000 cavalrymen. The Army of the Potomac, the Army of the Tennes-see, the Army of Georgia, 150,000 troops in all, passed in review welcomed by thousands of enthusiastic onlookers. Horace Porter, a personal aid to General Grant, marveled: "Vast crowds of citizens had gathered from neighboring States. During the review they filled the stands, lined the sidewalks, packed the porches, and covered even the housetops. The weather was superb . . . For two whole days a nation's heroes had been passing in review. Greeted with bands playing, drums beating, bells ringing, banners flying, kerchiefs waving, and voices cheering, they had made their last march." Indeed, with the final show of pageantry and military prowess, the seasoned veterans of Gettysburg, Shiloh, Cold Harbor, and Vicksburg were decommissioned, allowed to return home to peaceful pursuits but content with the knowledge that they had preserved the Union.

CHAPTER THREE
Washington Grows Up

After the long, glorious parade down Pennsylvania Avenue of the triumphant Union army veterans, Washington rapidly began to return to normal. Its citizenry eagerly anticipated the first summer in five long years without the bloodshed of a brutal military campaign. Determined to consign the memories of civil war to history, the area's defensive fortifications were abandoned to decay while the colorful bunting, flags, and other patriotic displays which had adorned every government building were torn down together with the last traces of mourning crepe. Peace had finally returned, Lincoln had been buried, and the Union was preserved.

Although the nation's capital had emerged from the war physically unscathed, it was nevertheless transformed by the conflict. The city's population had virtually doubled and now included a substantial population of freed slaves. Indeed, the last of the District's 1,700 slaves had been emancipated in 1862 while thousands of others had fled across Union lines to the safety of the federal capital. In hopes of easing the transition to freedom, Congress created the Freedmen's Bureau, entrusting the agency with "all subjects relating to refugees and freedmen." Under the able leadership of Major General O.O. Howard, the bureau's first task was to provide adequate food and shelter for newly emancipated slaves. In 1865 alone, over 31,000 rations of food were issued in Washington to help sustain its new citizens.

Since agricultural jobs were virtually nonexistent in the District of Columbia, several "Freedmen's Villages" were established in the area to provide assistance, shelter, and training to the former slaves. Ironically, one of the largest and most elaborate settlements was situated just across the Potomac River in Arlington on the antebellum estate of Confederate General Robert E. Lee. Arlington Village eventually became home to over 1,000 black residents who were provided with apprentice and vocational training. An article in *Harper's Weekly* described the freedmen's community as "quite lively, having a large number of children in it. For these there is a school house, there is besides, a home for the aged, a hospital, church, tailor and other work-shops, with other public buildings. The principal street is over a quarter of a mile long, and the place presents a clean and prosperous appearance at all times." During Reconstruction, the Freedmen's Bureau was credited with establishing well over 2,000 schools throughout the South and in the District of Columbia. Having been traditionally prohibited from learning to read and write by statute, young and old alike cherished the opportunity for education. Indeed, virtually all classrooms were filled to capacity with anxious, enthusiastic learners. In 1867, Howard University was chartered in Washington, D.C., as a black theological seminary. Named in honor of the director of the Freedmen's Bureau, the college initially enrolled only five students but, from this modest beginning, it has evolved into one of the country's premier black institutions.

Despite the diligent efforts of the Freedmen's Bureau, many blacks were still unable to find adequate employment or decent housing. Destitute and poor, hundreds were forced to seek shelter in Washington's notorious alley dwellings where tenements rented for modest fees but where conditions were ghastly, unsanitary, and overcrowded. One city report described conditions, "Whole families . . . are crowded into mere apologies for shanties . . . During storms of rain or snow their roofs afford but slight protection, while beneath a few rough boards used for floors . . . [is] the most disgustfully filthy and stagnate water . . . There are no proper privy accommodations." Despite such horrid conditions, the alley slums were sufficiently hidden from the public view and from the nation's conscience to remain a persistent and embarrassing problem for over a century.

One of the leading spokesmen against such injustice and inequity was Massachusetts Senator Charles Sumner. Through his personal intercession in Congress, District blacks eventually secured the right to serve on juries, testify in court, vote, and use public transportation. Still, these legal guarantees did little to overcome racism or ensure real equality. Many of Washington's white merchants and storeowners openly discriminated against blacks while others maintained an insidious system of dual pricing designed to discourage black patronage. Even most presidential inaugurations were segregated with separate galas held for black citizens the day following the more traditional revelries.

Politics continued to dominate the daily life of Washington during the post-war period. Area citizens were transfixed by each political scandal, feud, or intrigue. The new President, Andrew Johnson, provided ample entertainment. A man of limited education, Johnson lacked the political acumen of his predecessor, Abraham Lincoln. In fact, he managed to offend virtually the entire Congress by pardoning most Confederate soldiers and rebel leaders while attempting to run Reconstruction by executive fiat without the advice and consent of the legislature. A bitter feud soon developed between the President and Congress, culminating with the House of Representatives delivering nine articles of impeachment against Johnson in February 1868. He was charged with violating the spurious Tenure of Office Act and other "high crimes and misdemeanors."

The entire capital eagerly anticipated the President's trial in the United States Senate. Johnson, however, questioning the legality of the proceedings, refused to appear personally but his able team of lawyers offered a spirited and aggressive defense. Throughout the entire spring of 1868, Washington hotels and boarding houses were filled to capacity with reporters, politicians, and the curious. Each day, local newspapers printed elaborate and detailed accounts of the proceedings where the radical Republicans fiercely denounced Johnson as ". . . the [wretched] offspring of assassination" and derogatorily referred to him as "his accidentcy." Demand for the 800 Senate gallery seats was tremendous. Hundreds of people gathered at the Capitol each day, all anxious to gain admission to the chambers to witness the high

drama. Those fortunate enough to obtain a ticket eagerly took their seats and presence at the trial was seen as a sign of social status.

After weeks of testimony and debate, the Senate finally acquitted Johnson of all charges but only by a single vote. The President, angry and embittered, brooded out the remaining weeks of his term before finally ceding the office to Ulysses S. Grant in March 1869. The new Chief Executive, the great hero of the Civil War, arrived in a town that still consisted of unpaved streets, two story dwellings, and malarial marshes. *The Evening Star* in 1870 complained, ". . . our avenues remain unpaved; the [Washington City] Canal is useless and pestiferous; the old market sheds disgrace Pennsylvania Avenue; and Pennsylvania Avenue disgraces the city."

Alexander "Boss" Shepherd was appointed Vice President for Public Works in the District in 1871 and was determined to improve and modernize the capital. With great zeal Shepherd began a massive campaign to pave all of the city's roads. Under his supervision miles of sewers were also constructed and over 60,000 trees were planted. The old Washington Canal, long useless and inoperative, was finally backfilled. Simultaneously, the Army Corps of Engineers began extensive dredging operations in the Potomac River to deepen the channel to increase its current and improve navigation. Work on the Washington Monument was finally renewed and construction commenced on the Executive Office Building, the Smithsonian's Arts and Industry Building, and the Library of Congress.

In the late 19th century, many new, technological improvements were introduced to Washington. George C. Maynard established the National Telegraph Exchange, offering the first telephone service to the capital. A modest operation initially consisting of only 50 subscribers, the telephone exchange for the White House was simply—1; for the Capitol—2. Electrically powered trolley cars, street lights, and automobiles similarly helped transform the city so that by the turn of the century a contemporary guide book was able to proudly boast: "A wonderful change has been wrought in the past thirty years. Washington has developed into one of the most beautiful and attractive cities in the world . . . its public utilities have been placed upon the basis of the most modern methods, and its business interests have expanded greatly. The visible transformation is so striking as to excite the wonder even of inhabitants." Washington had truly emerged into a suitable capital for a great nation as the country approached what was expected to be America's century.

Library of Congress

With the end of the century, new ideas would begin to sweep the nation.

Mount Vernon

Just south of the capital in nearby suburban Virginia, is Mount Vernon the ancestral home of George Washington. The property, originally acquired by John Washington as part of a substantial 5,000-acre Northern Neck land grant, was far-removed from the prosperous plantations of the James River. Its remote setting, distant from the strategic international trade routes, prevented the property from being properly "seated" until the 1730s, when George Washington's father, Augustine Washington, finally erected a modest manor house and relocated his growing family to the plantation. The estate was originally named Little Hunting Creek but was later renamed Mount Vernon in honor of the heroic British Admiral Edward Vernon.

Ownership of the estate eventually passed to George Washington after the deaths of his father and brother. At that time, Washington was actively serving with the Virginia militia during the hostilities of the French and Indian War and was unable to reside regularly at the plantation. After his marriage in 1759 to the widow Martha Dandridge Custis, Washington wrote proudly that, ". . . no estate . . . is more pleasantly situated then this. It lies in a high, dry and healthy Country 300 miles by water from the Sea . . . on one of the finest Rivers in the world."

George Washington took an active role in the administration of the plantation. Like most Virginia planters, he was a large slaveholder, employing well over 200 slaves and overseers in the cultivation of some 15,000 acres of fertile Virginia soil. Initially, tobacco was the prime crop since it remained a profitable commodity despite international price fluctuations and excessively high labor costs. After assessing the severe soil damage caused by the crop, Washington wisely redirected his farm's entire resources toward the growing and harvesting of less destructive crops such as wheat, corn, hemp, and flax.

As political events in Virginia worsened during the 1760s, Washington was repeatedly elected to serve in the state's House of Burgesses in Williamsburg. There he became an ardent opponent of British colonial taxation policies and, in 1774, he was chosen to serve as a delegate to the First Continental Congress meeting in Philadelphia. The following year, Washington was appointed by the ensuing Congress as military commander of all the American forces fighting the British in Massachusetts. For the duration of the American Revolution, he was an infrequent visitor to his beloved Mount Vernon home, choosing instead to endure the many wartime hardships faced by his soldiers in the field.

After the return of peace in 1783, Washington quickly resigned his military commission and retired to his Virginia home. During the Confederation period that followed, Mount Vernon was a central stop for countless visitors who wished an audience with the General. All were graciously welcomed, entertained, and boarded. Once again, however, the numerous political and economic problems that crippled the nation's first government led Washington to public service. In 1787, he was chosen to serve as president of the Constitutional Convention which met in Philadelphia that summer. After months of deliberation and heated debate over the nature and ratification of the Constitution, Washington was elected the first President of the United States in 1789, an office which doomed him to reside in Philadelphia for the next eight years.

After completing two terms as President, Washington rejected all offers to run for re-election and retired once again to Mount Vernon, determined to assume the more genteel duties of a Virginia planter. Shortly thereafter in December, 1799 after working during a cold and snowy day, Washington became seriously ill. A local physician was summoned and attempted to purge the former President's system by bleeding him four times, but such efforts only further weakened Washington and he died on December 14, 1799. In his will, Washington expressed his desire to be interred in the family vault located on the Mount

An 1858 photograph of Mount Vernon, George Washington's ancestral home. The house was in a state of disrepair with one of its support columns missing. The Mount Vernon Ladies' Association acquired the property and restored it as a monument to the nation's first President.

Vernon estate and his remains were committed accordingly.

During the following year, First Lady Abigail Adams visited Washington's widow at Mount Vernon. The plantation had already entered a state of decline with Mrs. Adams later writing, ". . . the estate is now going into decay. Mrs. Washington with all her fortune finds it difficult to support her family." Just two years later, Martha Washington died and was buried next to her husband. Mount Vernon was inherited by a nephew, Bushrod Washington but the estate, still consisting of the mansion and over 4,000 acres of land, had ceased to operate on a profitable basis—its soil depleted and its slaves freed. By 1850, Washington's heirs had sold off all but 200 acres and the manor house, and they were desperately petitioning both the federal and state governments to purchase the property as a suitable memorial to the country's most beloved citizen. However, such acquisitions were without precedent and neither Virginia nor the federal government would assume responsibility for Mount Vernon.

Ann Pamela Cunningham, a South Carolina native, was appalled that such an important historic site had been allowed to fall into disrepair. She ambitiously created the Mount Vernon Ladies' Association with the expressed purpose of preserving the property. Funds were solicited throughout the country with thousands of school children donating a nickel to support the cause. Edward Everett, who would later gain fame as the featured speaker during the dedication ceremonies of the Gettysburg National Cemetery in 1863, was the most generous contributor providing $69,000 to the project. He justified his contribution stating, "While it stands, the latest generations of the grateful children of America will make this pilgrimage to [Mount Vernon] as a shrine; and when it shall fall, if fall it must, the memory and the name of Washington shall shed an eternal glory on the spot." Mrs. Cunningham's efforts raised $200,000, enough to purchase the property in December 1858. The manor house was meticulously restored and finally opened to the public. Seven hundred and fifty acres of land directly across the Potomac River on the Maryland shore were also purchased to prevent commercialization and to retain Mount Vernon's traditional serenity.

The Baltimore and Potomac Station

Washington's population showed dramatic increases in the decade following the Civil War, swelling to over 177,000 residents—a 42 percent increase in just 20 years. Simultaneously, local civic leaders were attempting to modernize and beautify the capital. Miles of gas pipes had been laid to provide citizens with indoor lighting and thousands of trees were planted along many of the city's newly paved streets. In the later 19th century, in an effort to prevent the construction of skyscrapers which many feared would darken Washington's streets and dwarf government buildings, the first height restrictions were put into effect limiting new structures to 13 stories. District health officials, dismayed by epidemic outbreaks of both tuberculosis and cholera, also ordered the backfilling of the old Washington canal and that new, clean water resources be made available to area citizens, many of whom were still dependent on public cisterns for water supplies.

New buildings were quickly replacing the old, dilapidated two-story structures typical of an earlier era. Most abandoned the city's distinctive classical-revival style, adopting instead the heavily ornamented Victorian architecture then in vogue. The new, red-brick Baltimore and Potomac (B&P) railroad station was typical of the new buildings. Located on the corner of 6th Street and Constitution Avenue (the current site of the National Gallery of Art), the ultramodern rail terminal was a welcome addition to Washington, providing passengers with spacious, comfortable waiting rooms along with a covered railroad platform which jutted 130 feet across the Mall. Only the nearby coal storage facilities and the rail yard detracted from the station's otherwise pleasant appearance.

On July 2, 1881, newly elected President James Garfield was scheduled to depart from the B&P terminal to attend his college reunion at Williams College in New England. Just 10 minutes before his departure, a deranged office-seeker stepped forward and shot the unguarded President twice. *The New York Times* reported, "President Garfield and Secretary Blaine drove from the Executive Mansion about 9 o'clock . . . to the depot of the Baltimore and Potomac Railroad, where the President was to join members of his Cabinet and proceed on a trip to New York and New England. As he was walking through the passenger rooms, arm in arm with Mr. Blaine, two pistol-shots were fired in quick succession from behind, and the President sank to the floor, bleeding profusely from two wounds. The assassin was instantly seized, and proved to be Charles J. Guiteau, a half-crazed, pettifogging lawyer, who has been an unsuccessful applicant for office under the Government, and who has led a precarious existence in several of the large cities of the country." The seriously wounded President was carried gently to the second floor of the terminal building where attending physicians probed his wounds. Secretary of War Robert Todd Lincoln, who had privately recounted the details of his own father's assassination to Garfield just two days earlier, lamented: "How many hours of sorrow I have passed in this town." After an hour, doctors summoned an ambulance to transport the President back to the White House. Once again, Garfield was carried through the terminal's waiting rooms now crowded with irate citizens and curious onlookers.

The assassin, Charles Guiteau, offered no resistance during his arrest. Several letters were confiscated from his possessions including one addressed to General Sherman which stated, "I have just shot the President. I shot him several times as I wished him to go as easily as possible." Another equally eccentric letter recounted, "The President's tragic death was a sad necessity, but it will unite the Republican Party . . . Life is a flimsy dream, and it matters little when one goes. A human life is of small value. During the war thousands of brave boys went down without a tear. I presume the President was a Christian and that he will be happier in Paradise than here. It will be no worse for Mrs. Garfield, dear soul, to part with her husband this way than by natural death. He is liable to go at any time any way. I had no ill-will toward the President. His death was a political necessity . . . I am going to jail." For the next several weeks, the President clung tenaciously to life while anxious citizens gathered daily around the White House to read posted bulletins concerning his condition. Herculean efforts were undertaken to comfort Garfield, including the installation of a primitive air conditioning system, where fans blew air over blocks of ice in an effort to lessen the draining effects of Washington's summer heat. Physicians, however, could do little to relieve the President's pain and discomfort and finally decided to allow him to recover at the New Jersey shore.

An American Express wagon was commandeered to transport President Garfield back to the B&P terminal. The road from the White House to the station

Library of Congress

The Baltimore and Potomac Railroad Station in 1881. The building is still draped with mourning crepe. The flag remains at half mast in tribute to President James Garfield who was fatally wounded by a deranged office seeker while at the terminal.

was covered with sawdust to lessen the strain while a special railroad car had been prepared for the journey, complete with a heavily springed bed and cooled with ice. The trip to Elberton, New Jersey, took an excruciating eight hours. Shortly after his arrival, the President was stricken by a fatal hemorrhage. He became the second American president to have been assassinated in Washington.

The nation's capital once again was draped in mourning crepe, including the B&P Railroad station which also flew a flag at half-staff. A special train returned the President's body to Washington

to lie-in-state in the Capitol Rotunda before final burial at the Lakeview Cemetery in Garfield's hometown of Cleveland, Ohio.

Guiteau remained confined in the District jail located in southeast Washington. He apparently was unmoved by the events and busied himself by selling his autograph for $1.00 to visitors and by writing bizarre pamphlets and letters. During his ensuing trial, the accused offered little defense and the jury sentenced him to death. On June 30, 1882, Charles Guiteau was executed in the prison courtyard.

The Ellipse

Before the 1860s, the land immediately south of the White House was undeveloped marshland, fed by Tiber Creek and frequently flooded by its overflow. Despite its early designation as a park for the President, the acreage was routinely used by District residents as grazing land for sheep and cattle herds, many destined for the slaughter-houses near the Washington Monument which served the Union army's insatiable appetite. In 1867, the government adopted plans drawn up by architect Andrew Jackson Downing to formalize the park. Roads were constructed and trees were planted to beautify the 32 acres which became known as the Ellipse. The unpredictable Tiber Creek was channeled underground through a series of sewage pipes to dry the area.

The close relationship of the Ellipse to the White House, made it an ideal location for public demonstrations. In 1892, the Grand Army of the Republic (G.A.R.) held its annual encampment in Washington, D.C. *The Evening Star* lamented, "The soldiers . . . are passing away. Year by year the number of those able to respond in body at a muster fast decreases . . . soon the last veteran will be gathered to his companions in arms." The elaborate week-long ceremonies brought together more than 80,000 former Union soldiers, including former President Rutherford B. Hayes and Generals O.O. Howard, Dan Sickles, and William Starke Rosecrans.

The encampment's central reviewing stands were erected on the Ellipse, and the park was used to bivouac some 15,000 G.A.R. members. The veterans' tents were carefully positioned to re-create the Union Army's positions during the final climactic campaign against Richmond. The central feature of the Ellipse display was a full-scale replica of the *Kearsarge*, the Union vessel which had sunk the Confederate blockade runner *Alabama* in a dramatic and fierce battle off the coast of France in 1864. Two small cannons mounted on the replica ship were used to sound reveille and taps each day.

The G.A.R. encampment was the precursor of countless other demonstrations on the Ellipse, from pacifists in World War I to Bonus Marchers during the depression. During the Vietnam War, over 100,000 anti-war demonstrators gathered in the park to express their opposition to President Nixon's ordered invasion of Cambodia.

There are numerous memorials located throughout the Ellipse. Nearest the White House is the unusual Zero Milestone. Dedicated in 1923 by President Warren G. Harding, the granite monument marks the original site of the beginning of a 1919 cross-country automobile trek to San Francisco. The Zero Milestone designates the exact site from which all highway distances to Washington, D.C. are currently measured.

Each December, the Ellipse is the scene of the lighting of the National Christmas tree and the accompanying *Pageant of Peace*, a tradition begun by President Calvin Coolidge in 1923. Initially, a new Christmas tree was cut each year and erected on the Ellipse only for the holiday period. In 1978, however, a living 35-foot Colorado blue spruce was planted and now serves as the permanent tree.

The Ellipse today is frequently used for sporting and recreational activities. It also serves the National Park Service as a staging area for public tours of the White House, a custom begun by President Thomas Jefferson in 1801 as a symbol of his belief in democracy.

The Grand Army of the Republic's encampment on the Ellipse, 1892. The aging Union Army veterans returned to Washington to recreate their triumphal 1865 march down Pennsylvania Avenue. A full scale replica of the ship Kearsarge *was the focal point of the festivities.*

The Executive Office Building

The early plans for the development of the city of Washington called for locating the major executive cabinet offices in the immediate vicinity of the White House. The Treasury Department was built in 1838 to the east, utilizing the typical classical revival style popular in the federal capital. To the west of the Executive Mansion were the Navy and War Department buildings, structures of undistinguished architecture but offices of vital importance during the Civil War. Secretary of War Edwin Stanton and his staff were located there and all official military communiques were channeled through the building. President Lincoln frequently walked the short distance from the White House to the War Department to learn the latest news from the battlefield and monitor other important dispatches.

After the war, both the Navy and War Department buildings were demolished to provide space for a larger and more utilitarian structure, the Executive Office Building (EOB). Construction continued from 1871 through 1888, resulting in a massive facility which would eventually encompass the Navy, War, and State Departments.

The Architect of the Treasury Department building, Alfred Mullett, had been commissioned to design the new EOB. The building, however, represented a drastic departure in architectural design, employing the Second Empire style which was then popular in France. Many Washington residents and government officials were horrified by the Executive Office Building's radical design and demanded that the newly completed structure be razed and replaced with a more traditional building. Many favored erecting an exact duplicate of the Treasury Department on the site to achieve architectural symmetry with the White House. The debate concerning the building's architecture raged for decades and was settled only in 1963 after President John F. Kennedy declared the building a historical landmark, an act which permanently ensured the building's architectural integrity and forever silenced those who advocated its replacement.

Interestingly, Mullett had used only granite and brick in the construction of the EOB in an effort to completely fireproof the structure. Even the elaborate interior cornices and door moldings were made completely from cast iron, painted to simulate plaster. In 1877, because of the building's relative safety from fire, the Declaration of Independence was moved to the EOB and placed on public display in the State Department Library. In an era of primitive preservation practices, the priceless document was unwittingly exposed to the harmful effects of sunlight and fireplace pollutants, seriously fading the Declaration's text and obscuring its signatures. In 1903, a special commission convened to safeguard the document. Its members recommended that the Declaration be perpetually stored in total darkness and ". . . never [placed] on exhibition." For the next 18 years, display of the Declaration was prohibited until the

National Archives

The Declaration of Independence on exhibit in the State Department Library at the E.O.B. The document suffered extensive damage during this time from sunlight and fireplace pollutants.

Admiral Dewey near the Executive Office Building in October 1899. The Executive Office Building, located next to the White House, was constructed entirely of granite, brick, and iron to completely fireproof the structure.

document was finally transferred to the Library of Congress into the custody of its staff of preservation experts.

During the century long history of the Executive Office Building, it has been the site of many notable events. After the attack on Pearl Harbor in 1941, the Japanese ambassador to the United States was summoned to the EOB by the State Department. Irate government officials formally issued the ambassador his "passport," a diplomatic order to leave the country. In 1955, President Dwight Eisenhower inaugurated the era of televised news conferences from the EOB's Indian Treaty Room.

Many prominent Americans have at one time maintained offices in the EOB, including Douglas MacArthur, John J. Pershing, and Theodore Roosevelt. After a 1929 fire damaged the west wing of the White House, President Herbert Hoover temporarily moved his executive offices to the building while repairs were made. President Richard Nixon frequently worked in a special office in the EOB which he felt afforded more privacy than the Oval Office.

With the expansion of the federal government during World War II, all cabinet offices were eventually moved to separate locations throughout Washington. Today, the EOB houses the Executive Offices of the President and the National Security Council as well as the Vice President's office.

The Key Mansion

In 1802, Thomas Clarke purchased a small tract of land overlooking the tranquil banks of the Potomac River. He began development of the property, undertaking the construction of a Georgian style mansion. After the improvements, Clarke sold the estate just three years later to an aspiring young attorney, Francis Scott Key, who used the residence to establish his George Town legal practice.

During the War of 1812, British forces seized Washington during a dramatic offensive. Most government buildings were destroyed during the brief occupation but the soldiers spared adjacent George Town. After abandoning the city, the British arrested a Maryland physician, Dr. William Barnes, who was taken onboard the frigate, *Surprise*, then anchored in the Chesapeake Bay.

Several friends of Barnes retained Francis Scott Key to intercede with the British for the doctor's release. The George Town attorney immediately travelled to Baltimore where he met with the ". . . illiberal, ignorant, and vulgar" British. Fin-

ally securing an agreement for the release of Dr. Barnes, Key was informed that he would have to remain on board a British warship because of impending hostilities against the American harbor defenses at Fort McHenry. Throughout the night of September 12, 1814, Key became an unwilling witness to the fierce naval bombardment of the American garrison. Despite the unrelenting British siege, the light of dawn revealed that the enormous garrison flag still flew defiantly above the fort. This scene so moved Key that he immediately composed a verse to commemorate the glorious victory. The poem would later be printed under the name, *The Star Spangled Banner,* and would be widely circulated throughout the United States.

Key ultimately returned to George Town where he continued to practice law from his M Street home. After the completion of the C&O canal, the area's provincial character changed radically. It was disrupted repeatedly by boisterous bargemen and drunken brawls. Key finally decided to sell his home in 1828 after accepting a position as the District Attorney for the city of Washington.

In the ensuing years, numerous entrepreneurs purchased the Key mansion, seeing the house as a promising site for business enterprise since it was located on one of only two roads into Virginia. Each new owner freely altered the building to accommodate their businesses which included a souvenir stand, an awning store, an ice cream parlor, a museum, and, appropriately, a flag factory. In 1912, the most drastic architectural changes were undertaken when the mansion's distinctive gabled roof was demolished and the building's facade was converted into a common store front. The alterations virtually destroyed the structure's architectural integrity. After President Herbert Hoover adopted

National Park Service

The Key Mansion, September 9, 1947. President Truman vetoed legislation to restore the building. It was later carefully dismantled to clear the site for a highway access ramp. The house was later "lost" after careless storage.

The funeral procession for the dead of the battleship Maine, *December 1899, en route to final burial ceremonies at Arlington National Cemetery. The Key Mansion, located on M Street, was once the home of Francis Scott Key, author of the Star Spangled Banner.*

Key's *The Star Spangled Banner* as the national anthem in 1931, the National Park Service acquired the mansion.

After World War II and a return to relative prosperity, Senator Robert Taft proposed legislation to fund a renovation of the Key Mansion which was in serious disrepair. President Truman, however, steadfastly opposed the funding, arguing that the building had little historical significance and that the earlier architectural changes had rendered it worthless. Furthermore, the President maintained that the nearby Key Bridge which spanned the Potomac sufficed as a monument to the author of the national anthem and promptly vetoed the Congressional bill authorizing the reconstruction.

In 1947, the construction of the elevated Whitehurst Freeway once again placed the Key Mansion in peril, as an access ramp to the Key Bridge necessitated moving the building. The National Park Service, in close consultation with the road contractors, painstakingly dismantled the house. The entire process was carefully documented with photographs and blueprints while the building's lumber and brick were carefully crated and numbered for an anticipated reconstruction. Sadly, no provisions for long-term storage had been made so the crates were merely deposited under the Key Bridge. After several years, the materials were dispersed throughout Washington, eventually misplaced or vandalized so that by 1981 all traces of the once majestic mansion had disappeared.

Center Market

The District of Columbia contained only modest amounts of arable land which began to vanish shortly after the creation of Washington. The encroachment of federal buildings and other incidental businesses further contributed to the paucity of farmland, as did the 1846 retrocession of 37 square miles of land to Virginia which was deemed surplus to the government's needs. Still, until 1880, many residents continued to live in rural areas of the District of Columbia. By that time, however, the city's residents were wholly dependent upon neighboring jurisdictions for food and dairy products.

Congress foresaw a need for centralized food distribution in the city. Indeed, immediately after the government occupied the city's federal buildings, farmers and other venders were permitted to set up stalls across from the President's House in Lafayette Square. The strong, unrelenting odors of the marketplace coupled with its unsightly spectacle led the government to order that the primitive market be removed eastward down Pennsylvania Avenue to a location at the key intersections of Indiana Avenue and 7th Street. The area soon became known as the Center Market and rapidly became a hub of business activity with taverns, hotels, printers, and apothecaries located nearby.

The market eventually spanned two city blocks and offered city residents ample supplies of vegetables, fruits, dairy products, and meat. A fish market used the stagnant, fetid waters of the old Washington City Canal to provide shoppers with live albeit tainted seafood. Even slaves could be purchased at Center Market until the Compromise of 1850 made such transactions illegal within the city limits.

Library of Congress

Farm wagons at Center Market, circa 1890. Fresh vegetables, fruits, meats, and fish were readily available to Washington residents.

Center Market was the focal point of Washington's commercial district during the 19th century. It was later demolished to make room for the National Archives.

In 1870, after the Civil War, Congress chartered the Washington Market Company and mandated that its directors upgrade the market's facilities. A new, impressive Victorian building was constructed on the site. It contained over 1,000 stalls for merchants and vendors. Likewise, farmers could park their wagons adjacent to the building to sell produce.

The market operated six days each week and became an important part of the lives of most Washingtonians. Constance Green writes in her book, *Washington: Village and Capital*, "On market day, elegant ladies descended from carriages driven by stove-pipe-hatted . . . coachmen and, trailed by a retainer carrying a basket, made the rounds of the stalls at the Center Market to select the fresh fruits and vegetables, the eggs and chick-ens, or the woodcock, wild duck, and other special delicacies of the season. There rich and poor rubbed elbows while chatting with the vendors and remarking on the weather to acquaintances. The true Washingtonian regarded marketing in person as much part of well-ordered living as making calls or serving hot chocolate to morning visitors."

As Washington continued to grow in the 20th century, Center Market began to face increased competition from rival markets and modern grocery stores. Coupled with the rapid growth of the suburbs and the desire of the government to "federalize" the central part of the city, Center Market was demolished in 1931. On the site, the National Archives was erected, now the official repository of the nation's documents and records.

The Washington Monument

Shortly after victory in the American Revolution, the Confederation Congress unanimously approved a proposal to erect a monument to George Washington. The original plans for the District of Columbia reserved a site at the end of the Mall for such a memorial. Bureaucratic delays coupled with the pressing problems of establishing a working government led to abandonment of the project.

In 1833, the Washington National Monument Society was founded with Chief Justice John Marshall serving as its first president. The organization, frustrated by the country's inaction, began to solicit funds for the long-awaited Washington Monument. Dozens of architects submitted proposals and drawings for the project which was awarded to Robert Mills. His design called for the construction of a towering obelisk surrounded by a Parthenon-style base which would house dozens

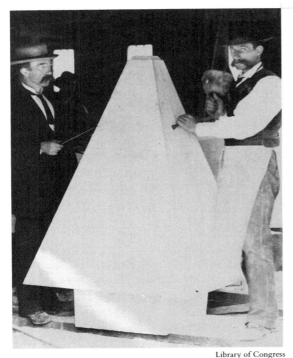

Library of Congress

The setting of the 3,300 pound capstone of the Washington Monument, December 6, 1884.

of statues of Revolutionary War heroes. Mills and the Monument Society hoped that Washington's heirs would permit the first President's remains to be transferred from Mount Vernon and entombed in a crypt that was planned for the memorial's base.

After carefully reviewing the plans for the monument, Congress ceded a tract of land on the Mall for construction. Located at the exact center of the original District of Columbia, the site was on the twin-axis lines between the Capitol and the White House. After the initial surveying was completed, however, the project engineers determined that the soil was too soft to support the weight of such an enormous structure. Consequently, the location was moved approximately 100 yards eastward and slightly disrupted the monument's relationship with the Executive Mansion.

On Independence Day, 1848, gala ceremonies were held for the setting of the cornerstone and the beginning of construction. House Speaker Robert C. Winthrop was the featured speaker. He delivered a 90-minute address followed by brief remarks by George Washington Parke Custis, Martha Washington's grandson. President James Polk and dozens of members of Congress attended the festivities, including the freshman representative from Illinois, Abraham Lincoln.

Progress on the obelisk proceeded rapidly and the structure soared to a height of 170 feet. In 1854, however, private funds for the project were depleted and work was suspended. The Monument Society made repeated appeals to Congress for government revenues but the petitions were rejected, subverted by growing sectional differences.

The Washington Monument remained a mere stump and a subject of derision. In 1867, Mark Twain wrote, ". . . [the unfinished monument] has the aspect of a factory chimney with the top broken off . . . cow sheds around its base . . . contented sheep nibbling pebbles in the desert solitudes . . . tired pigs dozing in the holy calm of its

Library of Congress

The dedication ceremonies of the Washington Monument, February 1885. Work on the memorial had been halted for over 35 years. When resumed, because of difficulty in matching the earlier marble, a distinct ring was apparent.

protecting shadows." After almost two decades of inaction, several Washington politicians began urging demolition of the memorial. The Monument Society had already abandoned the grandiose Parthenon-style base as part of its austerity measures but was still unable to raise sufficient funds to renew work. Finally, Congress assumed responsibility for completing the structure and ordered the Army Corps of Engineers to conduct a survey of the site. Additional concrete footings had to be set to support the weight of the obelisk and the finished height of the memorial was reduced to 550 feet. When construction was resumed, marble from the original quarries was unavailable. Despite efforts to match the earlier stone, a distinct ring was visible which forever marked the point where construction had been suspended.

On December 6, 1884, after 36 years of controversy and dispute, the 3,300-pound capstone was finally positioned at the top of the Washington Monument. The obelisk thereby became the tallest building in the world, a distinction it held until surpassed by the Eiffel Tower just five years later.

Dedication ceremonies were held, appropriately, on Washington's birthday in 1885. President Chester Arthur, nearing the end of his term, delivered brief remarks but the bitterly cold weather forced curtailment of the ceremonies. The completed obelisk was not opened to the public for three more years until a steam elevator became operational. The new device, however, was deemed so dangerous that only men were permitted to use it, leaving women visitors to climb the 898 steps to the top.

The Potomac Waterfront

The majestic Potomac River gently meanders for some 383 miles between the states of Maryland and Virginia before finally emptying into the Chesapeake Bay. The scenic river, navigable to the Little Falls just north of Georgetown, was a prime factor in the selection of a site for the federal capital. Indeed, in an era when overland transportation was either difficult or impossible, the Potomac promised relatively easy access to the seat of government as well as numerous commercial opportunities to sustain the city's resident population. Although several businesses did locate along the Washington waterfront, the capital never truly evolved into a significant port. It flourished only briefly during the artificial prosperity created by the Civil War, when the 6th Street wharves in Southwest served as a major debarkation point for federal soldiers. Further hindering its development was the emergence of both Baltimore and Norfolk as rival commercial centers. The two cit-ies, ideally located on the Chesapeake Bay, had naturally deep channels and superior harbor facilities far exceeding those of Washington, Alexandria, and Georgetown.

The Potomac River's commercial usefulness further declined after massive deforestation of the neighboring regions. The land, stripped of its naturally protective trees, suffered extensive soil erosion with each major storm. Tons of silt drained into the river, clogging the channel and hindering commercial traffic. The Long Bridge, the city's major span across the Potomac, also interrupted the regular cleansing tidal flow of the river necessitating regular dredging operations to clear debris. The city's notorious marshes and swamps with their high grasses and fetid waters accumulated further spoilage and provided fertile breeding grounds for malarial mosquitos. Stagnant water and contaminated wells caused epidemics of typhoid virtually every summer and led most lo-

An early view of East Potomac Park. Dredging operations are underway in the Washington Channel.

A winter-time photograph of the Washington wharves. Tour boats arrived here daily with passengers from southern Virginia and Maryland.

cal residents to abandon the capital during the hot summer months rather than risk the "Potomac fevers."

Attention to Washington's river problems was finally focused in February 1881, when a brutal winter and an unseasonable thaw caused severe flooding in the region. The Potomac's raging waters rose to within three blocks of the White House and threatened other government buildings. Congress ordered Major Peter Conover Hains and the Army Corps of Engineers to undertake substantive efforts to manage the Potomac's flow and to improve its overall water quality. Work soon began on dredging the river's channel and the massive amounts of silt and other waste materials were used to fabricate an artificial peninsula (East Potomac Park) that provided a protective harbor for Washington's wharves. The city's marshes were also drained and backfilled, thereby creating hundreds of acres of new land which Congress mandated would be "forever held and used as a park for recreation and pleasure of the people." To help improve the water quality, the Long Bridge was eventually replaced with a less obstructive iron span and a tidal basin was constructed with massive gates that could be opened at low tide to flush contaminants downstream away from the capital.

The Army's efforts to restore the waterfront helped revive many of Washington's river industries. Dozens of fish merchants and oystermen moored along the Washington channel and daily offered their catch to city residents. Tourists regularly arrived at the 6th Street wharves aboard ferry boats from southern Maryland and Virginia. Despite all of these 19th century improvements, however, pollution of the Potomac continued to be a serious problem with open sewers routinely emptying raw waste into the river. As late as the mid-1970s, the Potomac was deemed unsafe for fishing, swimming, and most other recreational activities until the federal government began conservation efforts once again to revitalize the river.

The White House

The White House, located at 1600 Pennsylvania Avenue, is the capital's most widely recognized landmark. The home of all American presidents since John Adams, the original building was designed by architect James Hoban. Work on the structure began in 1792 shortly after the chartering of the District of Columbia. On the earliest maps of the capital, the residence was titled, "the President's Palace," but widespread public outcry against the royal-sounding name resulted in designating the building simply, "the Executive Mansion." The term "White House," although in popular use throughout the 19th century, was not officially recognized until Theodore Roosevelt adopted it for use on his presidential stationary in 1901.

In November 1800, John Adams became the first president to reside in the Executive Mansion. He moved into the new building with a prayer that, "[God] bestow the best of Blessings on this House and all that shall hereafter inhabit it. May none but honest and wise Men ever rule under this roof." The First Lady, Abigail Adams, however, was distressed by the primitive conditions of the residence and complained in a letter that, "We have, indeed, come into a new country . . . The house is made habitable, but there is not a single apartment finished. We have not the least fence, yard, or other convenience outside. I use the great unfinished audience room as a drying room for hanging up the clothes! The principal stairs are not up, and will not be this winter . . . If the twelve years, in which this place has been considered as the future seat of government, had been improved, as they would have been if in New England, very many of the present inconveniences would have been removed."

President Adams was defeated for reelection shortly after moving to Washington and resided in the White House for only four months before returning to his home in Quincy, Massachusetts. The new chief executive, Thomas Jefferson, was a man of relatively modest tastes who scorned pageantry and ceremony. Under his administration, the White House was accessible to all citizens but the President's informal dress and rejection of protocol frequently offended the staid European diplomatic corps. They were often greeted by Jefferson while the President was clad only in a robe and slippers. Still, the President took an active interest in beautifying the mansion's grounds, personally drawing landscaping plans. On the south lawn, he had two earthen mounds built to break the monotonous view of the flat Potomac marshes and to simulate the rolling hills of the Virginia piedmont.

In 1814, the Executive Mansion was burned along with the Capitol and other government buildings by British soldiers. President James Madison and his wife, Dolley, desperately saved several of the mansion's most precious artifacts and relics before abandoning the city. Upon their return, Colonel John Tayloe hospitably offered his home, the Octagon House, on 18th Street as a temporary Presidential residence while the White House was rebuilt. It was not until 1818, however, and the administration of James Monroe that reconstruction of the mansion was finally completed.

Throughout the 19th century the mansion was regularly crowded with office-seekers, petitioners, well-wishers, and private citizens who wished an audience with the nation's First Citizen. Aleksandr Borisovich Lakier, a Russian noblemen who visited Washington in 1857, was shocked at the easy accessibility of America's highest ranking public official. He wrote, "You want to see the president and talk with him: if he is at home and not busy, you will be admitted without any special formalities or etiquette . . . if you were to enter the White House by mistake, not knowing who lived there, it would be difficult not to think it was a middle-class home." Even during the peak of hostilities in the Civil War, President Abraham Lincoln met with private citizens, referring to such encounters as his "public opinion baths."

The White House was unique among Washing-

The White House, July 14, 1911. Harry Atwood demonstrates a new Wright Type B airplane. The White House is unique in Washington, serving as both a private residence and an office building.

ton's government buildings since it continued to function as both a public office building and a private residence. Theodore Roosevelt, at 42, was the youngest chief executive in history. He brought to the White House a large family consisting of six young children who regularly roller-skated through the mansion's hallowed corridors, disrupted important cabinet meetings, and played throughout the house. An observer noted that, "Nothing was too sacred for [the Roosevelt children's] amusement and no place too good for a playroom." Compounding the problem was the children's menagerie of exotic pets which included raccoons, snakes, a bear, and a badger. When one of the boys was sick and confined to bed on the second floor, the other children cleverly brought their calico pony up a White House elevator for a sick bed visit.

With such domestic chaos, it was finally agreed in 1902 to add an attached west wing to the White House to provide "dignified office space" for the President. The mansion's greenhouse complex was razed to make way for the addition which upon completion housed the President's private office, a cabinet room, a lobby, a press room, and a telegraph facility. In 1912, the wing was further expanded under the direction of Nathan Wyeth. The President's office was redesigned into its characteristic oval shape and additional space was created for files, clerks, and the press. The White House was now able to function efficiently, ready to assume the new challenges of the 20th century.

Hotel W

CHAPTER FOUR
Washington Enters the 20th Century

In 1900, Washington, D.C. proudly celebrated its first 100 years as the seat of the government of the United States. An article in *Century Magazine* urged tourists, ". . . to come to help us fittingly celebrate the one-hundredth birthday of the nation's capital, Washington. The welcome will be heartfelt; the visit enjoyable; weather, everything, will be propitious, and the recollections thereof pleasant memories."

The District of Columbia had made vast improvements during the years following the American Civil War—the cobblestone streets had finally been paved with asphalt, most of the District's marshes were drained, and thousands of trees had been planted. Still, the splendid and grandiose capital that Pierre L'Enfant had designed and envisioned a century earlier had not been fully achieved. Instead, several recently built government buildings had completely forsaken the city's traditional classical revival style of architecture while the Mall remained cluttered with roads, trees, and railroad tracks. One contemporary author lamented, ". . . the Mall to-day is little frequented. It is almost waste grounds in parts." In 1901, Senator James McMillan was authorized by Congress to form a special commission to formulate a comprehensive plan for the future development of Washington. Charles Moore, the Clerk of the Senate committee, described the commission's function, ". . . the buildings shall be placed and the parks developed according to a definite system; and if this principle shall be established, the result must follow that the capital of the United States, already beautiful for situation, will stand as one of the most beautiful cities in the world."

The McMillan Commission hired some of the nation's leading architects, including Daniel Burnham, to develop proposals for beautifying the capital. The highest priority was given to the Mall since the key axis between the United States Capitol and the Washington Monument had been virtually obliterated. Over the next several years, due to the commission's efforts, the Mall was gradually cleared of the intrusive roadways, railroad tracks, and unsightly buildings. Final plans were also approved for construction of the long-anticipated memorial to Abraham Lincoln. The new classical style monument would serve as the logical western terminus of the reconstituted Mall.

First Lady Helen Herron Taft became actively involved in the early efforts to beautify the nation's capital. As an avid automobile enthusiast, she wanted to make the newly established Potomac Park, which had been formulated from silt and debris dredged from the river, into a scenic drive. Her plans were partially realized in 1912 when the Japanese government presented several hundred flowering Yoshino cherry trees to the city as a symbol of the everlasting friendship between the United States and Japan. Mrs. Taft and the Viscountess Chunda, wife of the Japanese ambassador, in ceremonies planted the first two trees along the Potomac Drive near the Tidal Basin. Shortly thereafter, the annual flowering of the Japanese cherry trees became an eagerly anticipated spring ritual in Washington.

The government was undergoing a major expansion during the early part of the 20th century. In 1912, Arizona became the 48th state admitted to the Union, completing American continental expansion. Victory in the 113-day Spanish-American conflict had led to the annexation of the Philippine Islands, Puerto Rico, and Guam, giving the United States colonial possessions and global responsibilities for the first time. The territorial growth of the country coupled with the establishment of a new American empire, led all three branches of the federal government to seek increased office space to carry out their ever growing responsibilities. At the White House, President Theodore Roosevelt authorized construction of a West Wing office complex. The Congress likewise funded two separate House and Senate office buildings on Capitol Hill. A new Supreme Court building was built on the site of the Old Capitol Prison allowing the justices to vacate their cramped chambers in the basement of the Capitol building for the first time.

The development and modernization of the federal government proved fortuitous. In 1914, the major European powers went to war. President Woodrow Wilson steadfastly proclaimed the neutrality of the United States in the conflict but after numerous provocations and attacks upon American merchant vessels by German submarines, Congress formally declared war on April 6, 1917. For the first time in history, the nation's soldiers were sent abroad to fight in a European conflict.

In Washington, emergency wartime mobilization led to the hasty construction of several temporary office buildings to accommodate the immediate need for office space. To help manage domestic resources, President Wilson appointed Herbert Hoover to head the wartime Food Administration. The agency urged Americans to aid the soldiers by voluntarily conserving food. Historian Thomas Bailey writes, "The Food Administration waged a whirlwind propaganda campaign through posters, billboards, newspapers, pulpits, and movies. Loyal citizens were urged to 'use all leftovers,' to observe 'the gospel of the clean plate,' and to practice 'the patriotism of the lean garbage can' . . . In order to save food for export, Hoover proclaimed wheatless Mondays and Wednesdays, meatless Tuesdays, and porkless Thursdays and Saturdays—all on a voluntary basis. Curious and unappetizing substitutes were found in wheatless bread ('Victory bread'), sugarless candy, and vegetarian lamb chops." President Woodrow Wilson proudly participated in all of the Food Administration's programs and conspic-

uously displayed one of the agency's stickers on a White House window. He also imported a flock of 18 sheep to graze on the White House's south lawn, keeping the grass trimmed and providing wool at the same time.

In Europe, the injection of thousands of fresh American troops into the war proved sufficient to break the prolonged military stalemate. After several successful Allied offensives under the command of General John J. "Black Jack" Pershing, an armistice in the war was finally declared on November 11, 1918. With peace restored and the war won, American "doughboys" were quickly returned to the United States. Many were granted a hero's welcome in Washington with a series of enthusiastic victory parades. The largest and most elaborate display was reserved for General John J. Pershing and 20,000 of his soldiers from the First Division. On September 17, 1919, an incredible 400,000 people gathered along the streets to glimpse the victorious commander and his troops. A special victory arch was constructed at the corner of Pennsylvania Avenue and 15th Street for the festivities.

Two years later, in 1921, Congress issued a resolution declaring Armistice Day a national holiday to mark the return of the American Unknown Soldier for burial at Arlington National Cemetery. The resolution read in part, ". . . this unknown soldier represents the manhood of America who gave their lives to defend its integrity, honor, and tranquility against any enemy." The interment ceremonies were held on the plaza of the Memorial Amphitheater with President Warren G. Harding presiding. He declared, "All America has halted to share in the tribute of the heart and mind and soul to this fellow American . . . it is fitting to say that his sacrifice . . . shall not be in vain . . . [and] that this Armistice Day shall mark the beginning of a new and lasting era, of peace on earth, good-will among men." The Commander-in-Chief during the Great War, Woodrow Wilson, was unable to participate in the Arlington ceremonies, and was forced to leave the funeral procession at the White House because of ill health. The former President had suffered a serious stroke during his final year in office and had retired to his home in Washington at 2340 S Street, N.W. President Wilson lived there until his death on February 3, 1924. He was interred at the Washington Cathedral, the only American President buried in the District of Columbia.

On March 4, 1929, after the uneventful six year presidency of Calvin Coolidge, Herbert Hoover, was inaugurated before an enthusiastic crowd of 50,000 people at the United States Capitol. Hoover proudly boasted, "The poorhouse is vanishing among us. We in America today are nearer to the final triumph of poverty then ever before in the history of the land." The inaugural parade that followed was particularly impressive because of the participation of 30 airplanes, four blimps, and the dirigible *Los Angeles* despite poor flying conditions.

Just seven months after Hoover took the oath of office preaching prosperity and fiscal health, the New York Stock Market collapsed on October 29, marking the beginning of the Great Depression. President Hoover was unjustly blamed for the economic disaster and throughout the remainder of his term, thousands of "hunger marchers" arrived in Washington to demand immediate relief and employment from the government. The largest and most prolonged demonstration, involved 20,000 veterans of the Great War who arrived in Washington in 1932 to appeal for early payment of a promised cash bonus. The so-called "Bonus Army" occupied several old, dilapidated government buildings along Pennsylvania Avenue and camped throughout the city in vacant lots. The demonstration proved to be a major embarrassment to Hoover who was then involved in the 1932 presidential campaign. In July, the United States Army was ordered to end the protest by evicting the demonstrators from government property. Mounted cavalry, armored tanks, and soldiers with gas masks and fixed bayonets marched menacingly down Constitution Avenue, hurling tear gas at the stunned veterans. The protestors were completely routed and forced to leave the city, but Hoover's slim chances for reelection collapsed as well.

Franklin Delano Roosevelt was elected in November and sworn-in as the 32nd President of the United States the following March. In his inaugural address delivered at the Capitol, Roosevelt declared, "This great nation will endure as it has endured; will revive and will prosper. So first of all, let me assert my firm belief that the only thing we have to fear is fear itself." He then called Congress into special session to enact his "New Deal" reforms which called for massive government employment to provide immediate relief to the nation's needy.

In Washington, the New Deal benefited thousands of area residents providing much-needed government employment. District residents were hired to work in the city's parks, to clean monuments, to index historical records, and entertain tourists. Despite Roosevelt's activist approach, the Depression lingered on through the decade but the very nature of American government had been irrevocably changed. Citizens now looked to Washington for both leadership and help in times of great national emergency and the most serious threat loomed ahead in 1941 when the survival of the republic would be at stake.

Library of Congress

A flock of Shropshire Downs sheep graze contentedly on the south lawn of the White House. The sheep helped keep the lawn trimmed during the war.

John Philip Sousa

In 1854, when John Philip Sousa was born in Washington, D.C., the nation's capital was still a provincial Southern town of just over 50,000 inhabitants. The city's lack of distinction was of little consequence to the young Sousa who fondly recalled his boyhood as a time of carefree fishing in the Potomac River coupled with the diligent study of the violin. The onset of the Civil War quickly transformed Washington into a city under siege, defended by thousands of young, patriotic Union troops. To Sousa, still only seven years old, it was a period of vivid memories full of the excitement and the spectacle of war with its parading troops, marching bands, and inspiring music. He later remembered, "As a boy I lived in Washington . . . the capital in those days was practically an armed camp. The days and nights were filled with marching troops, and the sight and sound of them left their impress on my youthful mind."

Sousa joined the Marine Corps band at the age of 13 but resigned after a brief enlistment to perform privately. He rejoined the Corps several years later and received an appointment as director of the service's band. Under his able leadership, Sousa and the Marine Corps band performed throughout Washington and were regularly featured at the White House. The band's concert repertoire included numerous patriotic pieces which mirrored the director's interest in native American music. Sousa was determined that the country's contributions to music be recognized and in 1891 compiled and published a comprehensive volume entitled, *National, Patriotic, and Typical Airs of All Lands*, which chronicled the history of American music.

Sousa once again resigned his commission in the Marine Corps to form his own touring band. His distinguished career and reputation as the "March King" gave the band instant credibility. They performed extensively throughout the United States, most notably during the gala quadricentennial celebrations at the World's Columbian Exposition in Chicago. The Sousa band also triumphantly toured Europe, performing before large audiences during 362 concerts in 13 countries, including a noteworthy appearance before the Tsar in St. Petersburg.

Throughout his long career, Sousa continued to write and compose many original musical scores including marches, operas, and waltzes. Among his most notable pieces were *Semper Fidelis*, *Washington Post March*, and *El Capitan*, a light opera. The most renowned of Sousa's compositions, however, was *The Stars and Stripes Forever*. Sousa himself acknowledged, "Of all my marches, I consider it the best, as it is the most popular." Humorist Will Rogers attributed the popularity of Sousa's music to the fact that ". . . [it] can quicken the blood, thrill the nerves of every American. His tunes [are] the Lincoln Gettys-

Library of Congress

John Philip Sousa

Library of Congress

John Philip Sousa conducting his band at Griffith Stadium, 1923. Sousa was a native Washingtonian and internationally known for his patriotic compositions including The Stars and Stripes Forever.

burg Address of music." John Philip Sousa dominated the American music scene for well over 40 years. In 1928, his expert testimony led to the adoption of Francis Scott Key's *The Star Spangled Banner* as the national anthem. Sousa persuasively argued that the piece, composed during the turmoil of the War of 1812 in a period of great crisis and adversity, was ". . . our best national air." In 1932, Sousa suffered a fatal heart attack while in Reading, Pennsylvania. The director's remains were returned to Washington for funeral services at the Marine Corps Barracks. Later, his flag draped coffin was placed upon a horse-drawn caisson and conveyed to Congressional Cemetery for committal. The *New York Times* reported, "John Philip Sousa was buried this afternoon in the uniform of a Lieutenant Commander of the Naval reserve with full military honors in Congressional Cemetery only a mile from his birthplace."

Sousa remains one of America's most beloved and revered composers. On each November 6, the composer's birthday, members of the Marine Corps band gather at his gravesite to honor their most renowned director. In 1987, Congress officially adopted *The Stars and Stripes Forever* as the national march of the United States. During testimony before a Congressional committee, Sousa's grandson stated, "For as long as I can remember, he has been an American institution, an American legend and, despite the fact that he died some fifty-five years ago, he and his music are as much a part of the national—and even world scene today as they were when he was alive . . . the "Stars and Stripes" [is] instantly recognized by anyone and everyone." Representative Morris Udall agreed commenting that Sousa's composition ". . . has become part of America. All agree that after the national anthem, there is no competition as a national song."

Union Station

The city that Pierre L'Enfant had envisioned in 1800—one with wide boulevards, magnificent monuments, and spacious parks—had only been partially realized a century later. Modern technology had slowly intruded with power lines, telephone poles, and railroad tracks, each significantly detracting from the city's innate beauty. In a concerted effort to remove dozens of unsightly buildings and other unattractive structures, Congress established the McMillan Commission with a mandate to transform Washington into a harmonious and elegant capital.

The commission began the metamorphosis by draining and filling many of the city's remaining marshes while simultaneously extending the banks of the Potomac River. Plans were developed to reestablish the key axis between the Washington Monument and the Capitol by clearing the Mall of trees, removing intrusive Victorian structures, and eliminating intersecting railroad tracks. The project required consolidation of the capital's two major rail lines and created a need for a centralized terminal. Daniel Burnham, the illustrious architect of the 1893 Columbian Exposition, was hired to design and build a suitable station, one that would be both utilitarian and serve as a fitting entryway into the nation's capital. Burnham creatively devised a building consistent with his monumental approach to architecture and one that would remain subordinate to the adjacent Capitol.

Work on Union Station began in 1903 and continued over the next four years. The terminal incorporated impressive Roman arches and classical statuary, and featured a massive central waiting room. The luxurious dining facilities, convenient ticket counters, and covered concourses provided travellers with modern comfort and convenience. Two massive 5,000-gallon water tanks, located on the roof of the station, provided running water throughout the building and also served as an unofficial swimming pool for engineers and train crews. A special Presidential Suite was reserved for the nation's "first passenger." After inspecting

the plush facilities, however, the Secret Service, mindful that James Garfield had been assassinated in a railroad station just two decades earlier, ordered that all of the glass doors and windows to the suite be replaced.

For the next 50 years, Union Station was the primary port of entry to Washington for visitors, politicians, and tourists. The terminal reached its peak usage during World War II after Congressionally mandated gas rationing forced most Americans to abandon their automobiles. Thousands of soldiers and sailors were detailed by rail through Washington en route to duty stations. The USO established special waiting areas exclusively for servicemen and issued special tags for them to wear so that hostesses could alert or awaken the soldiers in time to catch their connecting trains.

The ending of emergency war measures along with increased competition from airlines and automobiles crippled passenger rail service after the war. By 1960, Burnham's once magnificent station seemed antiquated and underused, continually plagued by leaky ceilings and crumbling plaster. Many argued that the terminal had become an anachronism and should simply be demolished. Congress still resisted such pressures and finally designated the station as the "National Visitor's Center" for the forthcoming Bicentennial celebrations. It was hoped that the funds appropriated for the conversion would reinvigorate the station. Repeated cost overruns, bureaucratic mismanagement, and the energy crisis cursed the project, and Union Station became an embarrassing symbol of government waste and maladministration. The multimillion-dollar National Visitor's Center consisted merely of a pathetic pit carved into the floor of the station's central waiting room and featured only a collage of flashing slides. Plywood barriers had been strategically positioned throughout the terminal to conceal the continued decay of the building. After only two years, the Bicentennial project was abandoned when Congress refused to commit any more government funds to save the station.

Union Station shortly after World War I. The railroad terminal was designed by Daniel Burnham and was the central point of entry for visitors to Washington for almost 50 years. The buildings in the foreground are dormitories constructed for female government workers during World War I.

In 1980, a torrential rainstorm severely damaged the station's roof and Congress was once again compelled to pay for emergency repairs. Shortly thereafter, a unique government-business venture was arranged which allowed for funding of the restoration and preservation of Union Station. In return, commercial businesses were allowed to rent space in the building and many new, elegant restaurants and chic shops were opened. Union Station once again became a thriving enterprise and a monument to the glorious days of the railroad.

World War I Washington

In 1913, on a typically cold and bitter March 4, Chief Justice Edward Douglass White administered the Presidential oath to Woodrow Wilson on the portico of the United States Capitol. Wilson was only the second Democrat to be elected to the presidency in 52 years.

After four years in office, President Wilson won reelection to a second term, campaigning effectively on the slogan, "He kept us out of war." Despite this pledge, repeated violations of American neutrality greatly exacerbated tensions between the United States and Germany, causing the President's second inaugural to be a joyless affair characterized instead by military displays and somber predictions. Less than one month later, Congress formally declared war on Germany and American forces began to mobilize and deploy across the Atlantic, joining the combined allied forces of Britain, France, and Russia.

Washington prepared for war. Entirely new government agencies and departments were created to administer and oversee the nation's effort. Temporary buildings were constructed along the Mall and throughout the city to provide desperately needed office space for an expanded federal bureaucracy. An urgent appeal for young women to come to Washington to assume jobs as clerks with the government was issued.

Despite the record number of apartment dwellings which had been built during the previous decade, the city was still unable to accommodate the influx of new residents. Boarding houses were filled to capacity and even the patriotic offerings by private citizens to lodge federal workers were not enough to answer the need. To help alleviate the shortage, Congress issued an emergency appropriation for the construction of 13 colonial style dormitories near Union Station for some 2,000 female clerks but the project was not completed until after the war.

In August 1917, Herbert Hoover was appointed Chief of the Food Administration and beseeched Washington residents to conserve crucial food resources. Hundreds of "Save Food" signs appeared throughout the District of Columbia, on storefronts and in trolley cars. Even the White House proudly displayed a "Food Administration" sticker in the window and the President diligently observed the mandated meatless and wheatless days which were regularly proclaimed throughout the war. First Lady Edith Bolling Wilson maintained a war garden on the grounds while President Wilson imported a flock of 18 Shropshire Downs sheep to graze on the south lawn, thereby keeping the grass trimmed and the White House gardener, Charles Henlock, annoyed. Henlock later recalled, "They were a nuisance, those sheep—but they were very pretty." The wool from the sheep was finally sheared and donated to the Red Cross which auctioned it off for $52,000.

Security against saboteurs and spies was a major concern in the District shortly after the declaration of war. The city's National Guard was dispatched to protect Washington's crucial water supplies and reservoirs while the President's security detail urged Wilson to curtail public appearances to lessen the chance of assassination. The greatest threat to the capital during World War I, however, was an invisible enemy, the Spanish flu. In September 1918, the city became virtually paralyzed by an outbreak of the illness which caused widespread absenteeism in all federal departments and wartime agencies. Despite orders that government clerks and employees be required to wear gauze masks to prevent the spread of the virus, the epidemic continued unabated. Area schools were closed, large public gatherings—including church services—were forbidden, and local theaters were required to suspend performances. Regional ordinances made it a misdemeanor to cough, sneeze, or spit in public without a handkerchief and there was serious talk of quarantining the entire city.

Congress issued yet another emergency wartime appropriation for one million dollars to be used to recruit doctors and nurses to the public health services. Volunteerism was encouraged in all sectors and, after the closing of the burlesque

President Woodrow Wilson patriotically leads a victory parade down Pennsylvania Avenue in 1919. An outbreak of the Spanish or "swine" flu proved to be the greatest threat to Washington during the war.

houses, even Flo-Flo and her widely admired chorus line, "the Perfect 36's," patriotically agreed to assist in an area hospital ward.

Over 12,000 people in the capital had documented cases of the virus during the first two weeks of October with 485 fatalities. Area morgues were filled to capacity and the city's morticians were unable to dispose of all the dead. *The Evening Star* noted that caskets were in short supply and that the public health agency had issued orders to ". . . prevent coffins [from] being shipped out of the District." One alert official noticed that a cargo of coffins destined for the Pittsburg area was passing through the city and confiscated the entire shipment. Nationwide, over 500,000 Americans, including 25,000 soldiers, died from the Spanish or swine flu.

Fortunately, the flu epidemic did not alter the final outcome of the war and on November 11, 1918, an armistice was signed bringing American involvement in World War I to an end. The nation immediately began to demobilize and initiated the process of returning American soldiers to the United States. In Washington, several victory parades were staged for the victorious "Doughboys," including a massive celebration for General of the Armies John J. "Black Jack" Pershing and his troops of the American Expeditionary Forces, a spectacle reminiscent of the grand march of the Union armies in 1865.

The Lincoln Memorial

Shortly after the death of Abraham Lincoln, several proposals were introduced in Congress to construct a suitable memorial to the martyred President to be located in Washington. Few, however, could agree to the size, shape, scope, or location of such a monument so, in frustration, the project was tabled. In 1911, the establishment of the Lincoln Memorial Commission with such notable members as President William Howard Taft, succeeded in resurrecting the project and final architectural drawings were prepared at last.

The commission recommended that the Parthenon-like structure be situated on the banks of the Potomac River overlooking Arlington National Cemetery on recently reclaimed marshland. The memorial would also serve as a new western terminus of the expanded Mall and would be connected to the Washington Monument by a reflecting pool.

Actual construction on the Lincoln Memorial began in 1914. A special rail line was built directly to the site to permit crates of lumber, marble, and stone to be unloaded on the grounds. Because of the soft, moist soil, 122 reinforced concrete piers had to be sunk to bedrock in order to support the massive foundation. For the next eight years, cranes and scaffolding surrounded the memorial as work progressed. In 1922, the dedication and transfer ceremonies were finally held on Memorial Day. Over 50,000 people gathered before the

National Archives

The dedication ceremonies for the Lincoln Memorial, May 1922. President Warren G. Harding delivered the keynote address. In attendance was Robert Todd Lincoln, the only surviving offspring of Abraham Lincoln.

The Lincoln Memorial under construction. The monument was built on reclaimed marshland and provided a western terminus for the Mall.

new monument to hear speeches and glimpse the various dignitaries, including President Warren G. Harding, Robert Todd Lincoln, and Chief Justice William Howard Taft. In his speech, Taft noted, "Here on the banks of the Potomac, the boundary between the two sections, whose conflict made the burden, passion, and triumph of [Lincoln's] life, it is peculiarly appropriate that [the Memorial] should stand. Visible in its distant beauty from the Capitol, whose great dome typified the Union which he saved, seen in all its grandeur from Arlington, where lie the Nation's honored dead who fell in the conflict, Union and Confederate alike, it marks the restoration of the brotherly love of the two sections in this memorial of one who is as dear to the hearts of the South as to those of the North."

The completed Lincoln Memorial had 36 Doric columns, each representing a state in the Union at the beginning of 1861 while above the colonnade were inscribed the names of the 48 continental states. Clearly the focal point of the memorial was the 19-foot statue of Lincoln sculpted by Daniel Chester French. It represented the wartime President, tempered by the burdens of the Civil War. Nearby were inscribed Lincoln's famous words from both his Second Inaugural and the Gettysburg Address.

An inspiring setting, the Lincoln Memorial quickly became a central gathering place for Americans seeking guarantees of their Civil Rights. Marian Anderson performed her famous 1939 Easter Concert from the memorial's steps and in 1963, during the 100th anniversary of the Emancipation Proclamation, over 200,000 people gathered on the grounds to hear Martin Luther King's "I have a dream" speech.

The Ku Klux Klan

During the summer of 1919, as thousands of American soldiers passed through Washington on their way home from duty in Europe, racial violence erupted in the nation's capital. Apparently sparked by a rumors of an alleged assault on the wife of a white sailor, dozens of marauding servicemen roamed throughout the southern sector of the city, randomly attacking black residents. Over the next few days, several people were killed during the racial unrest, prompting the mobilization of Washington's provost guard and troops from the Marine Barracks. While the military attempted to restore order, Congress denounced the riots as ". . . a national disgrace." Representative Frank Clark of Florida went on to charge that ". . . for the past month or so the capital of the nation seems to have been infested with the vilest criminals in all the land. Larceny, robbery, burglary, assaults of various kinds . . . have occurred within the shadow of the Capitol building itself."

Although peace was eventually restored, the Ku Klux Klan capitalized upon the climate of racial bigotry and relocated their national headquarters to Washington, occupying a building at 7th and I Streets. Under the leadership of Imperial Wizard William Joseph Simmons, Klan membership soared, peaking at 4 million during the 1920s, including some 15,000 members in the District of Columbia. The Klan's political influence increased correspondingly and the organization played a direct role in the election of 16 United States Senators and 11 state governors. In 1928, the Klan similarly was a major factor in orchestrating the defeat of the Democratic presidential nominee, Al Smith. Representative Thomas Ryan, distressed by the growth of the Klan, denounced the group before a Congressional hearing stating that: "Any organization that is anti-Catholic, anti-Jew, and against the foreign element in this country . . . is really a menace to this community."

In 1925 the Klan attempted to demonstrate its political strength by organizing a massive parade through the streets of Washington. Over 25,000 Klansmen from around the nation converged on the city. Many camped in parks near the Capitol while the Willard Hotel became the temporary headquarters for the march. On August 7, white-robed Klansmen proudly paraded down Pennsylvania Avenue. *The Washington Star* reported, "Abandoning their characteristic secrecy, today the vanguard of the Knights of the Ku Klux Klan poured into the Capital . . . in all their colorful regalia, but unmasked . . . marching with sturdy fortitude beneath a blistering sun . . . thousands upon thousands of supposedly untrained men, women, and children of the order wended their way in soldierly fashion along the humanity banked line of march."

After the parade, a number of Klansmen travelled to the nearby Arlington horse show grounds where a gigantic 80-foot cross was burned. Other members visited Arlington National Cemetery to place wreaths at the Tomb of the Unknown Soldier and on the grave of three time presidential candidate, William Jennings Bryan.

Despite the Klan's triumphal 1925 parade, the organization's avowed racism coupled with a litany of lynchings and other despicable acts of violence led to public disfavor. The very next year, an effort to duplicate the Washington march ended in dismal failure. A meager 15,000 returned for the 1926 parade which featured only two floats. One was described as a ". . . decorated motor truck on which several young women rode, one standing beside an American flag and holding in her hands an open Bible. The legend on the sides of the truck informed the onlookers that she was a '100 per cent American girl.'" *The New York Times* noted the parade's failure, stating that ". . . there did not seem to be nearly as much 'life' in today's parade as last year. The stepping was not as lively and the bands were not as numerous." With the end of the parade, so too ended a sad chapter in Washington's history.

In an unprecedented show of political strength, 25,000 members of the Ku Klux Klan march down Pennsylvania Avenue, August 1925. The Klan's national headquarters was located in Washington during this period.

The Great Depression

It was widely assumed in Washington that the presence of the federal government made the city virtually immune from the adverse consequences of economic recessions, financial panics, and fiscal crises. In the aftermath of the great stock market collapse of 1929, however, even the District of Columbia began to experience hard times. Mandated Congressional austerity programs dramatically slashed the federal budget, necessitating an 8% reduction in the bureaucracy. Furthermore, some government workers were required to accept involuntary furloughs without pay while others endured reduced work weeks. Salaries declined 23% from 1929 through 1933 while unemployment levels soared to a record high 25%.

Relief agencies and charitable organizations in the Washington metropolitan area attempted to lessen the negative effects of the Depression but the continual flow of protestors and demonstrators into the city strained their limited resources. Dozens of "Hoovervilles" comprised of small shanties and ramshackle shacks appeared along the outskirts of the city. Vacant lots were converted into small vegetable gardens, their harvest supplementing the meager diets of a population unable to afford the 35 cents a pound price for chicken let alone the $645 cost of a new 1935 Chevrolet. Each day, hundreds of destitute Americans, mostly jobless and homeless, gathered in protest in front of the White House or on the Capitol lawn, demanding a redress of their grievances from a seemingly impotent government.

In March, 1933, Franklin Delano Roosevelt was inaugurated as President, promising a "New Deal" for the American people while simultaneously demanding that Congress grant him ". . . broad executive power to wage a war against the emergency, as great as the power that would be given to me if we were in fact invaded by a foreign foe." With incredible zeal, various alphabet agencies were quickly devised to provide employment and immediate relief to the nation's citizenry. In Washington, thousands once again benefited from public employment with many working in projects to beautify the city. In 1934, for example, the PWA hired workers to scrub and clean the Washington Monument with steel brushes, soap, and water. Scaffolding was erected around the entire obelisk for the duration of the project. Meanwhile, numerous artists were commissioned to paint elaborate murals in government buildings while historians were employed by the WPA to produce a definitive guidebook of the capital. Still others were given jobs at the National Archives repairing damaged and torn documents with pressure-sensitive cellophane tape, a process which unknowingly only accelerated the deterio-

Library of Congress

One of Washington's notorious alley dwellings. Residents lived here without plumbing and in poverty and squalor. The Great Depression only exacerbated their hardships.

The cleaning of the Washington Monument by the PWA, October 18, 1934. President Franklin D. Roosevelt attempted to break the depression cycle by providing government jobs to the unemployed. This particular project took five months to complete and cost the federal government over $100,000.

ration. Along the Potomac River, choirs, orchestras, and bands regularly performed for residents and tourists, all through generous federal contracts. There was even a government-sponsored doll repair factory to restore children's toys.

Washington's black population suffered disproportionately despite all of the efforts of the Roosevelt administration during the Depression. They remained the victims of the twin evils of unemployment and segregation. Well over 50% of the city's black population were unable to find adequate employment while many others were channeled into custodial jobs. The District continued to operate a segregated public school system while many federal offices maintained segregated toilet and dining facilities. Theaters exiled blacks to "colored" balconies and the city's churches de-

nied the races the opportunity to worship together. Kelly Miller, a professor at Howard University, despairingly wrote, ". . . the destiny of the Negro population in large cities is clearly foreshadowed. The Negro population is to live and move and have his social being apart from the whites."

In 1934, the government's attention was once again focused upon the city's racially segregated slums. The Alley Dwelling Authority announced the ambitious goal of eliminating all such ghettos within the decade but, as the economic crisis deepened, such hopes proved illusionary. The final alley shanties were not demolished for another 40 years and as the 1930s ended, it was still possible to find poor, hungry, and destitute citizens living within the long shadow of the Capitol dome.

The Bonus Army

After the catastrophic collapse of the stock market in 1929, countless Americans became homeless and destitute. In 1932, over 20,000 jobless World War I veterans assembled in Washington to demand early payment of a bonus which had been promised to them by a previous Congress during more prosperous times.

Washington had graciously hosted previous demonstrations but the capital was ill-prepared and poorly equipped to handle a gathering of such magnitude and duration. Over 19,000 District residents were similarly unemployed and the area's social welfare services were already strained to the limits, lacking sufficient resources and revenues to provide additional food and shelter for the Bonus Army.

The veterans were forced to seek shelter wherever available. Many illegally took over a series of old, abandoned government warehouses along Pennsylvania Avenue which had been slated for demolition. Others encamped in the city's parks and vacant lots. The largest concentration of protestors was located on the Anacostia Flats at Camp Marks, home to 10,000 of the Bonus marchers. *The Evening Star* described conditions at the encampment, "There are shelters built of egg crates, of paper boxes, of rusty bed springs, of O.D. blankets, of newspapers, of scraps of junked automobiles, of old wall-paper, of pieces of corrugated iron roofing, of tin and bed ticking, of the rusty frames of beds, of tin cans, of rusty fence wire, of straw, of parts of baby carriages, of fence stakes, of auto seats. The man who can salvage an auto top from the dump has a mansion in this strange city." Major Dwight Eisenhower later elaborated, ". . . [the veterans] built miserable little shacks out of cast-off materials, tin cans and old lumber and the like—anything to shelter them from the rain and bad weather. Over outdoor fires, they cooked their scanty meals, sometimes a dozen veterans pooling all the food-stuffs they had to make a stew."

The Bonus Expeditonary Forces (BEF) were organized under the semiofficial command of ex-Sergeant Walter Waters. As a whole, the veterans were a well-behaved, disciplined group, their camps patriotically displaying dozens of American flags. Military order and decorum were maintained and many of the former soldiers spent their time drilling and marching. Each day, hundreds gathered on the Capitol lawn to petition Congress for payment of the bonuses. Boxing exhibitions were routinely staged at Griffith Stadium to raise funds to supplement charitable aid sent by sympathetic veterans' organizations.

In June 1932, legislation to fund immediate payment of the bonuses was overwhelmingly defeated by the Senate. The Congress adjourned a few weeks later, dooming all hopes of any further legislative action. The former soldiers, having no jobs or homes to return to, refused to leave Washington. Their continued presence became a major embarrassment to the Hoover administration and the protest was rapidly diminishing the President's meager chances for reelection in November. On July 28, the District Commissioners ordered the city's police to evict the veterans who were illegally trespassing on government property and to vacate the condemned buildings on Pennsylvania Avenue.

The Metropolitan Police accompanied by Treasury Department officials, arrived at the old warehouses armed with a formal eviction order. The veterans, unwilling to risk a confrontation, left without incident. Word of the government's action quickly spread to adjacent camps, and hundreds of Bonus Marchers converged on the scene. That afternoon, a small radical group skirmished with police. Several people were injured in the melee and one of the veterans was fatally shot.

Fearing that the disorders would escalate, 150 policemen were stationed around the White House and all gates to the mansion were locked shut. Regular army troops from Fort Myer were summoned to the scene and at 3 PM, a contingent of mounted cavalry under the command of Major George S. Patton crossed Memorial Bridge into the District. Augmented by six tanks and several

Camp Marks after the United States Army evicted the protestors. In the background is the U.S.F. Constitution, *docked at the Washington Navy Yard during the vessel's grand tour celebrating its restoration.*

hundred foot soldiers, the troops marched steadily down Constitution Avenue. General Douglas MacArthur, resplendent in full military regalia, conspicuously supervised the military action.

The BEF veterans stood passively by, more curious than belligerent. Their numbers had by now been greatly increased by hundreds of federal workers who had left their offices to watch the colorful spectacle. Major Dwight D. Eisenhower recalled that the Bonus veterans ". . . made no more vigorous protest than a little catcalling and jeering at the soldiers." As the infantry troops approached the Capitol, however, several bricks and rocks were hurled in their general direction. The army promptly responded with tear gas grenades and the rout of the Bonus marchers had begun. U.S. soldiers tore down the ramshackle villages and burned the rubble. Camp Marks was totally demolished leaving the veterans of the Argonne, Belleau Wood, and Verdun, stunned and dazed.

As the disheartened remnants of the BEF attempted to flee the city, armed police from Virginia and Maryland blocked all roads and bridges out of the District, each state unwilling to assume responsibility for the veterans. Only after the governor of Pennsylvania offered asylum to the marchers in Johnstown were the barricades withdrawn and the veterans allowed to pass through Maryland. Sergeant Waters bitterly denounced President Hoover, claiming that ". . . every drop of blood shed today or that may be shed in days to come as the result of today's events can be laid directly on the threshold of the White House."

For the next several weeks, dozens of Washington residents were given much-needed employment clearing the rubble of the 20 BEF camps which had been destroyed. Hoover's callous handling of the incident contributed to his humiliating electoral defeat by Franklin Delano Roosevelt, giving the marchers a small but empty victory.

Arlington Cemetery

In 1861, Colonel Robert E. Lee solemnly returned to his Arlington estate after refusing to accept command of the growing Union armies then being readied to quell the Southern rebellion. Lee, convinced that ". . . a Union that can only be maintained by sword and bayonets" was not worth preserving, left his plantation on April 22 to offer his services to the Virginia state militia. Meanwhile, General Winfield Scott, aware of the strategic value of the Lee estate with its commanding view of the nation's capital, ordered Northern troops to seize the property. On May 24, the plantation was occupied and its beautiful, classical revival manor house converted into a military headquarters for the Army of the Potomac. During the early months of the war, hundreds of Union soldiers were bivouacked on the estate. The troops freely foraged for materials that would help make their lives more bearable, denuding the property of fences, small trees, and other amenities. Radical alterations of the grounds were also ordered, including the construction of two defensive forts, Whipple and McPherson, to augment the expanding defensive perimeter protecting Washington from Confederate assault.

Library of Congress

The "Field of the Dead" at Arlington National Cemetery. Over 16,000 Union soldiers were buried on the former plantation of Confederate General Robert E. Lee during the Civil War.

The following year, the United States Congress passed legislation which effectively levied property taxes on all lands still claimed by the Confederacy. The Lee plantation in Arlington was assessed a tax of $92.07, a sum which Mrs. Lee rendered through her emissaries in 1864. The federal commissioners refused to accept the payment on the dubious grounds that the property owner had to appear personally. Shortly thereafter, Arlington was officially confiscated for tax default and sold to the federal government.

On June 15, 1864, the Quartermaster General of the Army, Montgomery Meigs, requested and promptly received permission from the War Department to designate 200 acres in the immediate vicinity of the Arlington House mansion as a national cemetery. That same day, 65 burials occurred on the grounds including several in the Lee's rose garden. By year-end, over 7,000 Union and Confederate casualties had been interred on the plantation, the graves marked only by rows of crude wooden tablets which seemingly stretched endlessly toward the horizon.

The Arlington estate had rapidly become uninhabitable as a private residence and after the war concluded, the Lee's abandoned all hopes of ever returning to their beloved home. Claim to the plantation ultimately fell to their eldest son, George Washington Custis Lee, who initiated litigation against the federal government, claiming that the wartime seizure of the Arlington estate was illegal. In 1882, the United States Supreme Court agreed ruling the government a trespasser and ordering that the Arlington estate be restored to its antebellum appearance. Rather than undertake the monumental and unpleasant task of disinterring over 16,000 soldiers, Congress agreed to compensate Custis Lee financially for the loss of the estate, thereby ensuring Arlington's continued operation as a national cemetery.

Over the next few decades, Arlington National Cemetery developed into the nation's most hallowed and cherished burial ground. In 1868, General John Logan set aside a day to decorate the

United States Army

The Tomb of the Unknown Soldier at Arlington National Cemetery. A large capstone was added to the monument in 1932.

graves of Union war veterans and to remember their sacrifice during the Civil War. The tradition evolved into Memorial Day and rapidly gained popularity as it was extended to other military cemeteries throughout the United States. In 1915, to accommodate the massive holiday crowds that annually visited Arlington on Memorial Day, construction of a new Memorial Amphitheater began. Shortly after its completion, in 1921 Congress approved plans for the interment of the American Unknown Soldier on its plaza. On Armistice Day, November 11, the third anniversary of the end of World War I, committal services were conducted.

The Tomb of the Unknown Soldier immediately became the focal point of Arlington Cemetery and the most widely recognized and revered shrine to American servicemen. Initially, it consisted of only a modest pedestal base until plans were adopted for a more elaborate and suitable monument in 1930. A 50-ton piece of Colorado marble was carefully positioned on the original structure and, for the next two years, work on the Tomb continued. Carefully sculpted into the front of the Tomb were three figures representing Peace, Victory, and Valor while on the facade facing the Amphitheater was etched the phrase, "Here Rests in Honored Glory, an American Soldier Known but to God." In 1937, the Tomb of the Unknown Soldier was placed under a continual military honor guard. Members of the 3d United States Infantry, "the Old Guard," assumed the vigil in 1948. Since the original burial, Unknowns from all of America's 20th century wars—World War II, Korea, and Vietnam—have been buried at the Tomb, with individual graves marked on the plaza by flat, white memorial stones.

Traffic

Public transportation was readily available to Washington residents as early as 1830 with horse-drawn omnibuses providing service to much of the downtown area. The rough cobblestones, however, made such trips so disagreeable that in 1862, in order to improve the overall quality of service, rail tracks were laid along Pennsylvania Avenue between the Capitol and the Treasury building. The new trolleys were still powered by horses and provided regular service at five-minute intervals for a fare of a nickel.

The city's trolley lines were finally electrified in 1888 by the Eckington and Soldiers' Home Railway Company. This modern, clean, and rapid form of public transit allowed for greatly expanded routes. By 1900 almost 200 miles of rail served the District and for the first time suburban jurisdictions were easily accessible. Neighboring towns such as Kensington, Chevy Chase, Falls Church, Arlington, and Alexandria, were all within an easy 35 minute commute of the city. Each of these areas thrived and enjoyed major population increases. Although service was now provided to the officially segregated states of Virginia and Maryland, Congress refused to allow "Jim Crow" cars on public trolley lines despite demands of suburban officials.

Just as the railroad had made canals obsolete, within a decade the automobile revolution had begun, dooming the city's trolley system. Mrs. A.L. Barber became the first District resident to buy and own a passenger car in 1897. At this time, most people still believed that the automobile was a mere novelty and few laws were imposed to regulate their use. In 1903, when traffic accidents began to mount, the city government mandated

Library of Congress

The corner of 14th and E Streets, N.W., July 1939. Washington's trolley system used underground power cables and remained in operation until 1962.

A typical Washington traffic jam, April 1937.

the licensing of operators, issuing some 858 permits that year. Soon afterwards, Congress imposed a rigid city speed limit of 12 miles-per-hour.

The first American president to ride in an automobile was Theodore Roosevelt. His successor, William Howard Taft, became an automobile enthusiast and purchased several vehicles for use at the White House. Still, tradition died hard and it was not until 1921 during the inauguration of Warren G. Harding that the car permanently replaced the horse-drawn carriage as the Chief Executive's principal mode of transportation.

During the 1920s, the suburbs continued to gain population and federal workers abandoned mass transit in record numbers, preferring instead the personal convenience of private automobiles. Daily commutes degenerated into an unremitting

struggle to find parking with government employees jousting with tourists for the District's limited available parking spaces. A federal study reported that ". . . the entire Mall has become an open-air garage." Massive traffic jams simultaneously plagued morning and evening rush hours, necessitating deployment of one-third of the entire Metropolitan Police force to traffic detail. Even the Depression era mandated government furloughs and staggered workshifts did little to alleviate the city's persistent traffic problems. Despite these realities, a government study proposing construction of a subway for the capital was rejected by Congress as too costly during a period of restrictive budgets. New highways and bridges were proposed, but only a world war could force Washingtonians to temporarily curb their passion for driving.

CHAPTER FIVE
Washington at War

On Sunday, December 7, 1941, the Washington Redskins were playing the Philadelphia Eagles at old Griffith Stadium. A crowd of almost 30,000 people had come to watch the football game, thankful for a brief respite from the grim news of repeated Nazi victories in Europe and stories concerning the collapse of delicate negotiations between State Department and Japanese emissaries. The fans' attentions were firmly focused upon the exciting and dramatic come-from-behind 20-14 Redskins' victory and few were even mildly distracted by the intrusion of an unusually large number of public address announcements for government leaders and military officials. After the game was over, however, the exiting crowd was confronted by swarms of paperboys in front of the stadium selling special edition newspapers which announced the Japanese surprise attack against American naval facilities in Pearl Harbor, Hawaii. World War II had finally come to Washington.

As word of the attack spread throughout the city, several hundred people began a solemn vigil in front of the White House. Most stood in stoic silence but a few individuals began to sing patriotic songs while a continual flow of automobiles entered the grounds with the President's key advisors, high-ranking military officers, and the Congressional leadership. Meanwhile, across town near Rock Creek Park, another group of citizens had gathered at the Japanese Embassy, angrily watching as the diplomatic staff hurriedly burned documents and records on the lawn.

The following day, December 8, President Franklin D. Roosevelt went to the United States Capitol to deliver a formal address to a joint session of Congress. After being enthusiastically welcomed with a bipartisan standing ovation by the representatives, the President began his remarks, "Yesterday, December 7th, 1941—a date which will live in infamy—the United States of America was suddenly and deliberately attacked by naval and air forces of the Empire of Japan." He continued by further denouncing the surprise attack on Pearl Harbor and chronicled numerous other Japanese atrocities. He finished his 13-minute speech, "No matter how long it may take us to overcome this premeditated invasion, the American people in their righteous might will win through to absolute victory."

After the President's dramatic speech, the Representatives and Senators adjourned to their separate chambers to deliberate on a war resolution. In the Senate, an act declaring war on Japan was quickly adopted by a unanimous vote of 82 to 0. In the House of Representatives, however, Congresswoman Jeannette Rankin of Montana, a confirmed pacifist who had voted against a similar measure in 1917, attempted to gain recognition to express her philosophical objections to the war. Despite Rankin's frantic appeal for a point of order, Speaker of the House, Sam Rayburn, steadfastly refused to recognize her. One fellow Congressman abruptly chided her, "Sit down, sister," and the vote proceeded. When the final result on the war resolution was tallied, the measure had passed by 388 to 1 with Congresswoman Rankin in sole disagreement.

The United States was now irrevocably committed to support the allied war effort and Washington, D.C. began the monumental process of mobilizing the nation while simultaneously organizing the country's defenses. Of utmost priority was the immediate need to protect President Franklin Roosevelt who was confined to a wheelchair. The United States Secret Service stationed heavily armed guards throughout the White House grounds and ordered that bulletproof glass be installed in the President's Oval Office. Likewise, a special gas mask was strapped to the President's wheelchair and one of the impenetrable vaults in the neighboring Treasury Department building was hastily converted into a makeshift bombshelter. The Secret Service also suspended the practice at the White House of flying the American flag when the President was actually in residence.

Throughout Washington, contingency plans

were rapidly being implemented to defend the city from potential enemy air raids. A strict blackout of all federal offices and monuments was enforced for the duration of hostilities while antiaircraft guns were strategically positioned on the roofs of many of the city's buildings. United States Army troops along with members of the District National Guard were dispatched to protect Washington's crucial bridges, water reservoirs, and public utilities from saboteurs.

The monumental logistics of fighting a two ocean war against both the Japanese and Germans combined with the necessity of raising a seven-million man army led to an unprecedented growth of the federal government. Entirely new government agencies and departments were being created daily to oversee war production, direct troop allocation, and systematize domestic rationing. An acute labor shortage soon resulted in Washington and threatened to slow progress toward victory in World War II. Consequently, the federal government began an emergency campaign to recruit young women to do their part for the war effort by leaving their homes to come to the capital and become "government girls." Most worked as clerks and typists during the wartime mobilization. As in World War I, the District of Columbia and surrounding suburbs had difficulty accommodating the large influx of new residents. Housing shortages became epidemic as the government hurriedly began to construct temporary barracks to shelter the new residents. In just two years, over 27,000 housing units were produced in the District. Despite such efforts, chronic shortages of affordable housing continued and local residents were encouraged to board wartime workers.

One of the most dominant aspects of wartime Washington was the imposed rationing of important commodities. Coupon books with minute stamps were required to legally purchase many common food items such as sugar, butter, and flour. Although there were periodic shortages of specific goods, most Washington residents patriotically attempted to conserve by growing victory gardens and using special cookbooks which

featured menus using only nonrationed items. With meat and chicken in short supply during the war, Atherton's Pet Shop creatively advertised for sale two ducklings for a price of 75 cents, promising, "They're a lot of fun and roast duck is hard to beat."

The gasoline rationing program was probably the most difficult to administer and the most frustrating for Washington's population. Ration cards were authorized based on a person's wartime job and particular needs. Area schools were temporarily closed to serve as distribution centers while school teachers were freed from classroom responsibilities to work as clerks. Long lines and endless delays ensued, angering many of the city's motorists who were forced to radically curtail their driving.

The Office of Price Administration became one of the largest wartime agencies, supervising and coordinating the various rationing programs while employing over 60,000 people. Richard Nixon worked at the OPA offices on Independence Avenue in Washington before enlisting in the United States Navy. Nixon later recalled, "The mission that I had was to develop the form letters and to write to thousands of people . . . to tell them why we could not give them an exception as far as their tire-rationing requests were concerned."

Throughout the war, bond rallies were held to solicit funds to support the war effort. Celebrities and movie stars frequently came to Washington to lend their personal support in the promotion of such drives. Numerous rallies were held at the Capitol, the Treasury Department, and other government offices featuring such notables as James Cagney, Lucille Ball, Fred Astaire, and Ronald Reagan. Scrap-metal collections were also common occurrences. James Goode writes in his book *Capital Loses*, "[Scrap iron] drives were intensified in 1942, the year in which the United States lost enormous quantities of ships . . . to German submarines. More than 40 tons of scrap metal were donated by Washingtonians that year. The usual items given for the scrap-metal drives consisted of old water tanks, lawn mowers, toasters, vacuum cleaners, typewriters, safes, shovels, washing machines, pans, electric fans, and iron beds." In 1942, there was still serious discussion among federal leaders concerning the possibility of using many of the city's bronze statuary and monuments for scrap. Fortunately the generosity of the District's citizens was sufficient to make such dramatic action unnecessary.

By early 1945, victory in both Europe and the Pacific seemed likely. President Franklin Roosevelt was inaugurated for his fourth term in office on the South Portico of the White House on January 20 with only a few thousand invited guests in attendance. The abbreviated ceremonies, necessitated by Roosevelt's poor health, included a six minute Presidential address and lacked the grandeur and pageantry of earlier inaugurals. Indeed, he died only a few months later while on a trip to Georgia on April 12, 1945, ironically on the same day American and Soviet forces were linking up at the Elbe River in Germany for the final wartime offensive in Europe. The news of the President's death stunned the nation's capital. Stores and businesses closed immediately in Roosevelt's honor and many display windows featured black bordered portraits of the deceased President. When the body arrived at Union Station, it was met by the new President, Harry S Truman, who accompanied the coffin back to the White House. Over 500,000 people lined Pennsylvania Avenue to glimpse the funeral procession and pay their respects to the nation's former Commander-in-Chief. Truman later remembered, "The streets were jammed. People on both sides of the streets when we brought the body back, people were crowded together, and people were crying. I saw one old . . . woman sitting down on the curb with her apron up to her eyes just crying her eyes out." Roosevelt was later buried at his home in

Hyde Park, New York, and the final stages of the war were now entrusted to Harry Truman, a relatively unknown politician from Missouri.

In Europe, the German army had completely collapsed and Adolf Hitler and much of the major Nazi leadership committed suicide. Formal surrender finally came on May 8, 1945, and Truman declared victory in Europe, VE Day, but still cautioned, "[This is] a solemn but glorious hour . . . Much remains to be done. The victory won in the west must now be won in the east." Indeed, the recent campaigns against the Japanese on Iwo Jima and Okinawa had been the most costly and bloody of the entire war while the anticipated invasion of Japan, itself, was expected to cost an additional one million American casualties. For the first time since 1941, however, the United States Capitol was again illuminated, the threat of air raid having long since passed.

Throughout the summer, American combat troops were being redeployed from Europe to the Pacific theater in preparation for the final assault on Japan. On August 6 President Truman announced that a new "atomic bomb" had been dropped on Hiroshima. Three days later, a similar device obliterated the city of Nagasaki, compelling the Japanese to surrender unconditionally on August 14. After four years of vigilance, the nation's capital erupted into joyous celebration as the streets filled with government workers and soldiers. President Truman declared, "This is the great day . . . the day when fascism and police government ceases in the world . . . the day for the democracies." As the celebrations continued, few people in Washington were concerned about the future, a period which would pose new challenges for the nation and another conflict just as dangerous.

The Roosevelt Bunker

After the Japanese surprise attack on American naval facilities in Pearl Harbor, Hawaii, the federal government undertook massive emergency preparations to defend the nation from further hostile enemy action. The crippling of the U.S. Pacific fleet was seen by most government officials as a mere prelude to massive bombing raids against American cities similar to the *blitzkreig* that had effectively destroyed Warsaw and which was currently being waged against London.

The United States Secret Service, the agency charged with protection of the President, immediately doubled the number of agents assigned to its White House detail. A new, impenetrable iron fence was erected around the grounds to prevent foreign agents from launching a suicide attack against the President. To establish an effective defensive perimeter around the White House, the grounds were closed to public visitation and several new, specially constructed guard boxes were strategically positioned at all entrances. East and West Executive Avenues were sealed off to traffic while a contingent of Army soldiers from Fort Myer were assigned to patrol and secure the area. Heavily armed Secret Service agents were posted within the mansion itself to prevent unauthorized access to the President. '

The crisis atmosphere that prevailed immediately following the United States' declaration of war on Germany and Japan led military strategists to urge President Roosevelt to authorize the camouflaging of the White House to reduce the danger of an air attack. It was further proposed that the building's slate roof be painted black and the traditional white walls covered with a subdued color. Roosevelt, however, resisted such counsel and agreed only to draping the executive mansion's windows with heavy blackout material. He also consented to the installation of bulletproof glass in the Oval Office and the moving of his desk away from its traditional window location. Agents were allowed to strap a gas mask to the President's wheelchair for his use in the case of a chemical attack.

There remained an urgent need for the construction of a permanent White House bombshelter under the East Wing. Such construction, would require several months, during which time the President would be unacceptably vulnerable to enemy air attacks. The Secret Service decided to create a temporary shelter in an existing vault located in the adjacent Treasury Department building. Agents secretly commandeered vault #1, removing its contents of seven million dollars worth of narcotics and over 700 million silver dollars. In an effort to make the new bunker more inhabitable, drapes were used to cover its plain, white walls and carpets were quickly placed over the hard concrete floors. A command center equipped with 12 telephone lines was established with desks that converted into beds for the President's staff. A spartan office and bedroom were set up for the President and ample amounts of canned food and bottled water were stockpiled.

To provide further protection for the invalid President, a 741-foot long underground passageway was constructed between the White House and the Treasury bunker. Built in a zig-zag design to lessen the chance of a direct hit by an enemy bomb, work on the tunnel commenced just six days after Pearl Harbor and proceeded literally throughout the day and night. Tons of excavated dirt were removed from the construction site and routinely dumped on the grounds of the Washington Monument. After completion, Roosevelt personally inspected both the tunnel and the bunker facility but neither one was ever used by the President during the war. The only official use of the facilities occurred when British Prime Minister Winston Churchill used the tunnel to elude reporters while on a trip to Washington.

After World War II, the Roosevelt bunker in the Treasury Department was dismantled and the vault returned to its more traditional use. The permanent bombshelter built under the East Wing and the tunnel between the White House and Treasury Department, however, still remain.

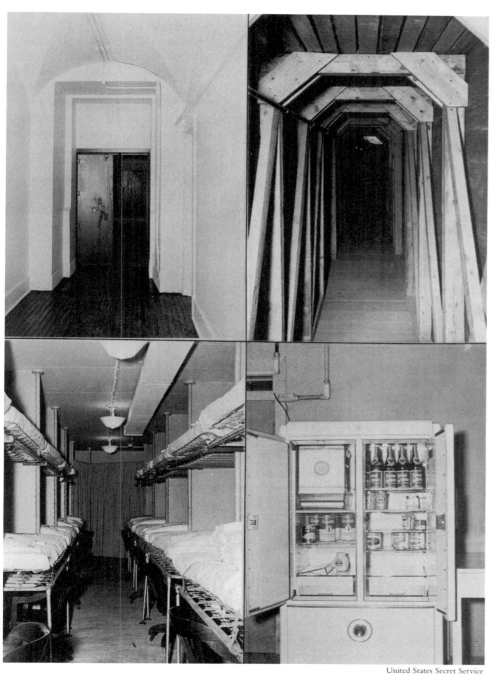

United States Secret Service

President Franklin D. Roosevelt's bunker in Vault #1 of the Treasury Department Building. Roosevelt, confined to a wheelchair, was extremely vulnerable to enemy action or possible assassination. Extraordinary precautions were taken during the war to ensure his safety.

The Defense of Washington

After the stunning successes of the Imperial Japanese forces against Pearl Harbor and throughout the Pacific, it quickly became apparent that the United States was vulnerable to further attack and even potential invasion. The nation's capital was virtually defenseless, unprotected from enemy air raids, traitors, saboteurs, and fifth columnists. In an effort to lessen the immediate danger, hundreds of Army troops from Fort Myer were sent to the city to guard crucial water reservoirs and other public utilities. World War I era machine gun emplacements were hastily erected near all of the Potomac bridges to protect the spans from possible espionage. NBC news correspondent Bryson Rash recalled, "After Pearl Harbor, by nightfall, you had army personnel around the White House grounds with armored cars. The second thing they did was put anti-aircraft guns and army personnel on the railroad bridge across the Potomac, at Fourteenth Street, and started laying a pontoon bridge. It seemed incredible, but that bridge was the only railroad link between North and South east of Harper's Ferry, West Virginia. If saboteurs wanted to really bother you, they could nave blown up that railroad bridge."

In the anger and hysteria that followed Pearl Harbor, some misguided citizens chopped down four Japanese cherry trees located near the Tidal Basin which had been presented as a token of "everlasting friendship" by Japan. Despite the hostilities and the Japanese treachery, there was little support in the city for such mindless acts of vandalism. The Superintendent of the National Capital Parks Office, Irving Root, vehemently condemned the action as a malicious and unwarranted ". . . destruction of beauty in the national capital."

There was a sense of urgency that pervaded the capital during the early days of the war. Because additional enemy air raids seemed to be a real possibility, Congress issued emergency orders which extinguished for the duration all spotlights used to illuminate the Capitol, the White House, national monuments, and other federal facilities. Local civil defense wardens were dispatched to police the District's streets to enforce citizen compliance with regulations mandating the use of blackout curtains on all windows. Simultaneously, city planners quickly dissected the city into civil defense districts to coordinate rescue and firefighting operations while local students in suburban areas had air raid drills incorporated into their daily routines. Young school children at the District's Bancroft School were required to wear identification tags for their protection in the case of enemy attack.

There was also an immediate concern for the safety of priceless government documents. Archibald MacLeish, the Librarian of Congress, was worried that a surprise enemy attack could destroy many of the nation's most important historical records and artifacts. He contacted the United States Secret Service to arrange for the transfer of several such items to the gold vaults of Fort Knox. Secret Service Director Frank Wilson organized the shipment which included the Constitution, the Declaration of Independence, the Articles of Confederation, the Gettysburg Address, and Lincoln's Second Inaugural Address. He later remembered, "We decided to transport [the documents] from the Congressional Library to Union Station in an armored truck under guard of Secret Service agents. At the station the boxes were placed on a Baltimore and Ohio train . . . the priceless documents were delivered to the Fort Knox depository and placed in Compartment No. 24 . . . only five people in Washington and two and the gold depository in Fort Knox were aware that these historic documents had been secretly transferred to what I considered the safest place in the United States."

By early 1942, the military had strategically positioned a series of antiaircraft guns on buildings throughout Washington. Some of the emplacements, however, were merely harmless replicas designed to fool enemy spies and agents but the vast majority were armed, manned, and ready. As the war gradually turned in favor of the allies,

An antiaircraft gun on the Department of the Interior Building. A gun crew on the building accidentally fired one of the guns and struck the Lincoln Memorial, slightly damaging the Maryland State seal located on the monument's frieze.

some of the gun crews became less vigilant. Indeed, one machine gun emplacement located on the roof of the Interior Building was accidentally fired, the bullets striking the Lincoln Memorial, causing minor damage to the marble but fortunately no loss of life. Despite such setbacks, the capital was finally prepared to repeal any aggression.

Wartime Rationing

Shortly after the initial shock of Pearl Harbor, the federal government quickly initiated emergency plans to mobilize the economy. The Office of Price Administration (OPA), an agency that would eventually comprise over 60,000 workers, was entrusted with overseeing the rationing of some 20 crucial items as well as curbing speculation and thwarting black market activity. Gasoline and rubber were among the first commodities in short supply as German submarine activity disrupted the flow of such imports.

Motorists were initially implored to conserve; speed limits were lowered to 35 mph—"Victory Speed." Leon Henderson, the chief administrator of the OPA, urged Americans to curtail pleasure driving, carpool to work, use public transportation, and ride bicycles. In a widely circulated photograph, Henderson was pictured riding his "Victory" bike to his Washington offices, his comely secretary proudly perched on the handle bars and various staff members following close behind. By

National Archives

The War Price and Rationing Board, December, 1942.

May 1942, it had become apparent that voluntary conservation was inadequate to support the war effort and mandatory rationing was imposed.

In the District of Columbia, classes were suspended in the public schools for three days to make the buildings available as distribution points for gasoline ration cards. Teachers were ordered to serve as clerks while students enjoyed the imposed holiday. The program for the city's 125,000 drivers established a tiered system ostensibly based upon need and occupation. "A"cards were provided to nonessential workers and allotted only three gallons per week while the coveted "X" card gave the bearer the right to purchase unlimited amounts of gasoline. First Lady Eleanor Roosevelt received her "A" card during a highly publicized White House press conference but most members of Congress ignored her example and instead demanded and received the "X"cards, despite predictable public outrage.

For Washington area citizens, lines began to form at the area's schools hours prior to the scheduled openings of the distribution centers. Meanwhile, other motorists jammed the city's filling stations, trying to horde as much gasoline as possible. *The Evening Star* reported, "The drain on [gasoline] supplies was so great today that many station operators had to choose between instituting an informal rationing system on their own, or letting pumps run dry. Four hundred motorists had been turned away from one station in the Northwest section by noon. Others were limiting sales to 50 cents, or two gallons . . . Long lines of cars waited at nearly every station, and many dealers expected soon to shut up and go home."

During the entire three days of the program, rationing lines stretched for blocks. At Central High School, one administrator commented that he had ". . . never seen so many people in one place." The enormous demand caused spot shortages of cards and emergency supplies had to be rushed to some distribution centers. Despite occasional outbursts of temper and verbal abuse, the program generally operated smoothly. In Wash-

The line at Coolidge High School for gasoline ration cards, May 13, 1942. Washington motorists were urged to curtail pleasure driving during the war and to conserve other vital resources.

ington, fully 12% of all applicants received the "X" card and its unlimited supplies of gasoline compared to just 1% nationally.

Many residents in the metropolitan area, unable to get tires, spare parts, or enough gasoline, simply abandoned their cars during the war, consigning them in special lots for "frozen" vehicles while others attempted to sell their automobiles. In Arlington, Eva Belle Mimms wrote to her husband, 2nd Lieutenant Leroy Mimms, in East Anglia, England, of her intent to sell the couple's 1937 Chevy Deluxe at a price well above the car's market value. Lt. Mimms, fearful that wartime production would make new private automobiles unobtainable for months after a return to peace, quickly sent a "V-mail" letter vetoing the idea.

Several food items were also among rationed commodities in the Washington area. Sugar, flour, and meat were routinely in short supply but specially published wartime cookbooks featured many unique recipes for sugarless cakes and other delicacies that used only nonrationed items. Victory gardens helped alleviate some of the hardships and the capital's thriving black market offered the unpatriotically ample supplies of virtually all commodities including ham at $1.25 per pound and nylon stockings at $5.00 a pair. Still, the American homefront, organized and managed by the massive Washington bureaucracy, proved to be a crucial part in the nation's overall war effort. Throughout the war, inflation was kept in check and U.S. soldiers well supplied. The nation had won its domestic battle.

The Wartime Housing Shortage

The logistics of waging a two-ocean, global war transformed Washington into a massive and efficient headquarters of a superpower. The federal bureaucracy was expanded to an unprecedented level, exceeding even the emergency measures necessitated by the Great Depression. New federal agencies, regulatory commissions, and other government departments were created almost daily to manage a multimillion-man Army, track wartime casualties, organize the homefront, and establish war production goals.

With most of the nation's young men enlisted in the armed services, an acute labor shortage occurred throughout the nation jeopardizing production in industries, farms, and other vital businesses. In Washington, there was an urgent need for clerks, typists, and secretaries to staff the federal bureaucracy. The government eliminated civil service entrance exams and aggressively began to recruit young women from across the nation to travel to the capital to serve as wartime "desk warriors." Over 280,000 patriotic young Americans heeded the call, most arriving at Union Station with little more than a suitcase and the promise of a $1,440 per year civil service job.

With the start of the war and the massive influx of population, a chronic shortage of both office space and rental housing developed in Washington. Within three weeks of the Congressional declaration of war, dozens of construction crews were deployed around the city assembling prefabricated buildings along the Mall. These utilitarian, barrack-like structures could be completed from foundation to occupancy in just over five weeks and had the effect of immediately transforming the capital's landscape. The government temporaries seemed to appear miraculously, carelessly interspersed between memorials and monuments with wartime necessity clearly taking precedence over architectural tradition.

The newly arrived government workers, likewise, were in desperate need of affordable rental housing. Local hotels, already filled to capacity with visiting dignitaries and foreign emissaries, restricted room rentals to just three days and were often forced to set up beds and primitive sleeping arrangements in lobbies and hallways for disgruntled guests. The Navy Department built a series of barracks for female military personnel in West Potomac Park adjacent to the Lincoln Memorial. Elevated, covered walkways were built across the Reflecting Pool to connect the buildings with the central Main Navy and Munitions complex. Just across the Potomac River, other military housing facilities were erected on the grounds of the old Arlington Experimental Farm on land which has since been appropriated for grave space by Arlington National Cemetery.

With boardinghouses and apartment buildings in the District mandating multiple occupancy, local construction firms urged patriotic citizens to attach wartime room additions to their homes. Washington residents once again responded, with many offering vacant rooms in their houses to government employees. In Arlington, Virgin-

National Archives

Wartime workers arrive at the Fort Myer South Post in Arlington, Virginia. In the 1960s, the land was annexed by Arlington National Cemetery and converted to grave space.

Temporaries located along the Reflecting Pool during World War II. Hundreds of the prefabricated structures were built during the war throughout the city. The Main Navy and Munition facilities located along Constitution Avenue, however, dated to World War I. The barracks for WACS and WAVES in West Potomac Park were built after Pearl Harbor and were connected to the Navy complex by two covered, elevated walkways.

ia, Eva Belle Mimms was typical, renting a bedroom to a local school teacher. Meanwhile, suburban jurisdictions suspended local zoning ordinances to allow the rapid construction of entirely new, low rent apartment complexes. Vacant lots were also turned into instant trailer park communities for government workers.

The influx of these wartime residents forever transformed the capital and the federal bureaucracy. They were the nameless army who tirelessly generated the paper pronouncements, decrees, and documents which helped win the war.

The Pentagon

On the eve of World War II, the United States military hierarchy was widely dispersed throughout Washington, D.C. in 17 separate locations. The lack of a centralized, coordinated command structure proved inefficient and tended to accent interservice rivalries—a dangerous combination with the approaching hostilities with Japan and Germany. General Brehom Burke Somervell became the leading proponent for construction of an entirely new, self-contained military headquarters to be located in Washington which would house the offices of the Secretaries of War and Navy as well as those of the major military commanders of each of the armed services. Such a building, Somervell believed, would help facilitate the drafting of an effective response to Axis aggression while simultaneously improving communications among the Navy, Marine Corps, Army, and Coast Guard.

The proposal for building the Pentagon was presented to President Franklin D. Roosevelt who favored the concept in principle but had several key reservations concerning the actual design, cost, and location of such a massive facility. There were virtually no satisfactory sites within the District of Columbia. The location favored by the military was currently occupied by old Washington Airport adjacent to Arlington National Cemetery. Many critics, including the Chairman of the Commission on Fine Arts, Gilmore Clarke, feared that such a building would detract from the cemetery's beauty and disrupt the symmetry of the capital. Clarke argued, "We think [the Pentagon] would be one of the most serious and worst attacks on the plan of Washington that has ever been made."

The Arlington site, however, had many distinct advantages. The Washington Airport had become outdated, equipped with only one rustic terminal, a dilapidated hanger, and a single runway intersected by a highway. With the opening of the new, modern National Airport just to the south, the commercial airlines had already ceased using the facility making the land available for purchase by the federal government. Likewise, the area was conveniently located to Washington with ample space to accommodate not only the Pentagon itself, but also the necessary parking lots. As a result, the Arlington site was finally approved by the administration but with the stipulation that the Pentagon be restricted to five stories to ensure that the view from Arlington Cemetery would remain unobstructed and that planes using National Airport could operate in safety.

President Roosevelt had initially favored designing a new command headquarters without windows to bombproof the structure in the event of an enemy air raid. However, the military was able to persuade him to abandon the idea because such precautions would do little to protect the structure and would pose monumental engineering problems. With the last of the obstacles removed, construction on the Pentagon finally began in August 1941. Initially, some 14,492 concrete pilings had to be carefully sunk into the soft ground to support the massive foundation of the building. As world tensions worsened, work on the Pentagon was given the highest priority and was authorized to continue on round-the-clock basis. Incredibly, the entire building was finished in just over eight months. *The Evening Star* re-

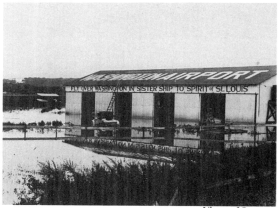

Library of Congress

The old Washington Airport, 1923. The airfield became obsolete with the opening of the new, modern National Airport and was torn down for the Pentagon.

National Capital Planning Commission

The Pentagon, circa 1945. The military headquarters was built in just over eight months and remains the largest office building in the world with over 17 miles of corridors.

ported, ". . . the War Department's mammoth Pentagon Building in Washington [is] the capital's most fabulous new sight."

Secretary of War Henry Stimson moved his office and entire staff from the old Executive Office Building to the Pentagon in April 1942. Shortly thereafter, President Roosevelt and his aide, Harry Hopkins, were invited to tour the impressive new facility. When the President questioned the need for the unusually large number of restrooms, he was informed that Virginia segregation laws required separate accommodations for white and black employees. The state's segregation policy, however, was never implemented.

The Pentagon, built with five concentric rings,

immediately became the largest office building in the world complete with 17.5 miles of corridors but, because of the building's efficient design it was possible to reach any part of the building in just 17 minutes. During the peak war years, over 33,000 people worked at the Pentagon. It was also the most heavily guarded building in Washington. Once after 86 Pentagon employees suddenly became seriously ill, there were fears of sabotage and infiltration by foreign agents. Fortunately, the outbreak was quickly traced to food poisoning caused by spoiled salad dressing and butterscotch pie served in the Pentagon cafeteria. The mystery was solved and the efficient prosecution of the war continued.

The Washington Navy Yard

Personnel at the Washington Navy Yard took great pride in the production of the massive 16-inch rifled guns they produced for the nation's 15 commissioned battleships. The impressive weapons were capable of hurling a one ton shell over 20 miles and had made the American battleship Navy the most impressive and powerful fleet in the world. Navy Yard workers were astonished at word from Pearl Harbor that four of the ships had been sunk and an additional four heavily damaged during the Japanese air raid of December 7, 1941. They immediately began preparations to help the fleet recover from this catastrophic defeat.

The Washington Navy Yard traced its origins

United States Navy

The production of 16-inch naval guns at the Washington Navy Yard. The facility was involved in the production of weapons and ordnance until the beginning of the war. Later, it became a major research and development installation.

back to 1799 when the United States was engaged in an undeclared naval war with France. During that time, defenseless American merchant vessels were routinely seized by French warships in clear violation of United States neutrality. President John Adams and members of his Federalist Party urged a major buildup of the United States Navy in an effort to deter further French belligerence and Congress finally appropriated sufficient funds to build six new 74-gun ships-of-the-line, several frigates, and adequate support facilities.

The Secretary of the Navy Benjamin Stoddert, directed that one of the recently funded Navy yards be built in the uncompleted federal capital and personally selected a 40 acre site along the Anacostia River. Construction of docks and support buildings began under the direction of Benjamin Latrobe, the architect of the Capitol, who also designed the installation's distinctive main gate. The Navy Yard rapidly developed into one of the capital's most important industrial enterprises, employing over 300 men in shipbuilding, maintenance, and repair work. Virtually all of the ships in the Navy's small fleet, including the *U.S.F. Constitution* and *U.S.F. Constellation*, were serviced there during the years prior to the War of 1812. During the war, however, the entire yard and all of its buildings were intentionally destroyed by order of the commandant Captain Thomas Tingey to prevent the strategic facility from falling into enemy hands during the British occupation of the District in 1814.

The Washington Navy Yard was rebuilt after the Treaty of Ghent formally brought hostilities between the United States and Great Britain to an end. The reconstructed yard continued to expand and develop during the post-war period, notably establishing the first marine railway in 1822. After the outbreak of the Civil War in 1861, the Washington Navy Yard became a critical naval installation repairing Union gunboats patrolling the Potomac River. Likewise, federal ships involved in maintaining the blockade of the Confederate coast

American warships docked at the Washington Navy Yard, October 1945, shortly after the Japanese surrender.

United States Navy

were often serviced there. President Abraham Lincoln enjoyed visiting the Navy Yard to discuss the war with the officers and crews of the Union vessels docked there. On April 14, 1865, Lincoln and his wife took a carriage ride to the Navy Yard and toured the monitor *Montauk*. The ship's surgeon, Harry P. Todd, wrote in a letter, "Yesterday about 3 PM the President and his wife drove down to the Navy Yard and paid our ship a visit, going all over her accompanied by us all. Both seemed very happy, and so expressed themselves, glad that this war was over, or near its end, and then drove back to the White House." A few hours later, President Lincoln was shot at Ford's Theater. His assassin, John Wilkes Booth, escaped into southern Maryland across the Navy Yard Bridge located to the east of the facility.

After the Civil War, the nation demobilized most of its naval armada and the Navy Yard's importance declined correspondingly. In 1886, the installation was converted into the principal gun and armament factory for the Navy. By the turn of the century, the yard, now known as the Navy Gun Factory, was thriving and employed some 2,225 people in the production of ordinance and armaments to fulfill President Theodore Roosevelt's pledge to build a "Navy second to none." During World War I, the Navy Gun Factory produced an average of 469 guns per year, including the famous 16-inch naval batteries which were mounted on specially built railcars for infantry use.

The bombing of Pearl Harbor mobilized the entire nation in support of the war effort. Production of ordinance and the manufacturing of weaponry were consigned increasingly to private industry. As a result, the Navy Yard and the gun factory were assigned to direct research and development of new weaponry rather than actual production. Unique captured Japanese, German, and Italian guns were often sent to Washington for analysis by naval experts stationed at the yard. Through their work, many crucial wartime devices were developed which helped win the war against the Axis Powers.

Wartime Diversions

Throughout the United States, World War II was serious and grim business. In Washington, thousands of GIs regularly passed through the city before being shipped abroad. Other returning veterans arrived to receive treatment of war wounds or convalesce at Bethesda and Walter Reed Hospitals. Each day, several identical flag draped coffins were delivered to Arlington National Cemetery for burial, a solemn reminder to the citizens of Washington of the desperate battles raging in both Europe and the Pacific.

Washington civilians and wartime workers were urged to help win the war with constant appeals to conserve food, participate in salvage drives, curtail driving, and work extended hours. Celebrities and movie stars likewise came to the city to publicize and solicit funds for war bonds. In Washington, their efforts combined with such slogans as, "They Give Their Lives—You Lend Your Money," "Back the Attack," and "Lend Over Here Till It's Over Over There" successfully raised millions of dollars for the war effort.

Despite the stark and ever-present realities of World War II, the District was still an exciting and interesting place to visit. Soldiers-in-transit would often use a portion of their leave to spend a few extra days sightseeing in the nation's capital. With most hotels already filled to capacity, servicemen generally were boarded at one of several USO facilities, places where they could relax, listen to music, write letters, and socialize. Local guidebooks, which listed the capital's many historic and notable sites, were readily available. Many publications offered advice as to where a soldier could meet one of the city's many single women.

Local hotels served cocktails for just 30 cents a drink and most establishments also enticed customers with live orchestras and dancing. The Shoreham on Connecticut Avenue advertised dinner and a show for just $2.50 per person while the Wardman Park Hotel offered an evening of intimate dancing in its Metronome Room to the music of Leonardo and his orchestra. For American servicemen who preferred more exotic form of entertainment, the Gayety Burlesque Theater on 9th Street featured comedian Eddie "Nuts" Kaplan and headlined the "glorified burlesque" of Hinda Wassau and her Hinda Belles.

Probably the most popular diversion in wartime Washington was the movies. In the spring of 1943, several local theaters were showing the popular *Road to Morocco* starring Bing Crosby, Bob Hope, and Dorothy Lamour. At RKO Keith's *Frankenstein Meets the Wolf Man* with Bela Lugosi and Lon Chaney offered the adventurous ". . . titanic mayhem in the night." Lest the movie-goer forget, war bonds could be conveniently purchased in the lobbies of most theaters.

Glen Echo Amusement Park in nearby Maryland was also a popular form of recreation. Easily accessible from downtown by trolley, the park offered 40 acres of attractions, free admission, and nightly dancing from 9 PM to midnight. One Glen Echo advertisement in *The Evening Star* stat-

Library of Congress

American servicemen and their dates relax at Glen Echo Amusement Park in suburban Maryland, April 1943. The park claimed to be "the favorite Washington playplace."

National Archives

A group of American servicemen and their companions enjoy the spring and the flowering of the Japanese cherry trees. Shortly after Pearl Harbor, four of the trees were vandalized by irate citizens. The Jefferson Memorial was the only major Washington monument completed during the war, dedicated by President Roosevelt in 1943.

ed, "To the new residents of Washington seeking diversion from their usual duties, Glen Echo Park is the ideal recreation center. It provides relaxation so much needed in these strenuous times. The older residents of Washington and vicinity know Glen Echo as the favorite Washington playplace."

During the spring and summer months, professional baseball remained a popular pastime despite the war. The Washington Senators who played at Griffith Stadium, historically languished in the cellar of the American league and was a team whose limited talents were further decimated by the wartime draft which claimed many of their star players. Still, each season, the ever-optimistic manager of the Senators, Ossie

Bluege, promised area baseball fans an elusive winning season. Starting times, however, dictated by mandatory blackouts, were in the mid-afternoon when few wartime workers could be spared from their jobs causing a sharp decline in attendance.

Despite the many wartime diversions available to soldiers and residents in Washington, the capital still remained dedicated to total victory. The work of war always took precedence; however romantic strolls along the Tidal Basin near the newly completed Jefferson Memorial, visits to the National Zoo, or just enjoying the many sites of the capital offered a needed respite from the business at hand.

The Axis Embassies

Ambassador Kichisaburo Nomura preferred the pleasant accommodations at the Hotel Washington to those of the Japanese Embassy located near Rock Creek Park at 2514 Massachusetts Avenue. At the hotel, Nomura was conveniently near the Executive Office Building where he regularly met with the American Secretary of State Cordell Hull concerning the strained relations between the Empire of Japan and the United States. By the fall of 1941, Imperial Japanese forces had successfully conquered Manchuria, subdued much of China, and were rapidly subjugating the rest of Southeast Asia. The Roosevelt administration, furious over the brutal Japanese aggression in the region and their blatant territorial ambitions, had attempted to punish the island nation with a strict embargo of all U.S. steel and scrap iron exports. The economic policy did little to deter the Japanese. The sense of impending disaster was heightened with the arrival in Washington of Special Envoy Saburo Kurusu in November 1941.

Diplomatic negotiations were at an impasse on December 7, when the Imperial Japanese fleet launched a surprise attack against the American naval base at Pearl Harbor, killing 2,500 American servicemen, destroying 200 airplanes, and crippling 5 battleships. At 2 PM EST, after the assault on Hawaii had been successfully completed, Kurusu and Nomura arrived at the State Department with a belated communique severing all relations between the United States and Japan.

As news of the bombing of Pearl Harbor spread throughout Washington, about 200 people gathered in front of the gate of the Japanese Embassy, silently watching as members of the embassy staff hurriedly burned piles of secret documents, code books, and other records on the lawn. The Metropolitan Police were summoned and arrived shortly thereafter but were powerless to stop the destruction of the documents because of the embassy's privileged diplomatic status. The State Department promptly issued a formal release stating, "Immediately upon receiving news of the Japanese attack upon Hawaii, the American government took steps to see that absolute protection was accorded the Japanese official establishments and official personnel within the jurisdiction of the United States."

Ambassador Nomura and Special Envoy Kurusu were ordered confined to their rooms at the Hotel Washington. Other Japanese personnel were restricted to the embassy compound until an agreement guaranteeing the return of all American diplomats abroad could be arranged. The following day, President Franklin Delano Roosevelt addressed a joint session of Congress to request a declaration of war against Japan.

On December 11, Nazi Germany and Fascist Italy declared war on the United States as predicted by the State Department. The President sent a written message to Congress stating, "The forces endeavoring to enslave the entire world now are moving toward this hemisphere. Never before has there been a greater challenge to life, liberty,

National Archives

Inside the German Embassy, May 1945. The end of an era.

State Department officials removing the sign for the German Embassy, May 1945. After VE Day, the embassy no longer had any diplomatic identity and could thus be seized by government officials.

and civilization . . . Rapid and united effort by all of the people of the world who are determined to remain free will insure a world victory of the forces of justice and of righteousness over the forces of savagery and of barbarism . . . I therefore request the Congress to recognize a state of war between the United States and Germany, and between the United States and Italy."

At the German Embassy near Thomas Circle, the staff began to burn all secret documents and communiques. Baron Ulrich von Gienanth, a member of the SS assigned to the embassy, calmly informed a crowd of American reporters that he intended to return to Germany at once and request a combat assignment. Meanwhile, diplomats at the Italian Embassy on 16th Street were attempting to sell their private automobiles but

were informed by the FBI that the Treasury Department had frozen all Italian assets because of the hostilities. Federal agents also sealed all hostile embassy compounds to prevent anyone from entering or leaving the grounds.

By early 1942, virtually all diplomats from belligerent nations had been expelled. The embassies of the warring countries were placed under the protection of the neutral Swiss government for the duration. Once the war was over and all of the Axis powers had unconditionally surrendered and thus lost all diplomatic identity, the State Department confiscated the buildings and their contents. Most of the incriminating documents had been destroyed previously and all that was left were mere curiosities and artifacts of the doomed totalitarian regimes.

ZERO MILE
STONE POINT
OF DISTANCES
FROM WASHING
TON ON HIGH
WAYS OF THE
UNITED STATES

CHAPTER SIX
Washington After the War

Harry S Truman enjoyed taking a brisk walk through the streets of Washington despite the persistent objections of the United States Secret Service. He usually agreed to be accompanied by only a single agent but was routinely followed by a crowd of anxious reporters and photographers. As he strolled through the city, enjoying its historic sites and the opportunity to talk with its citizens, Truman would often pass through the Ellipse just south of the White House and by the Zero Milestone. The marker, from which all highway distances to Washington were measured, took on added significance during the the tensions of Cold War by symbolically marking ground zero in the nuclear age.

After victory in World War II, the wartime alliance between the United States and the Soviet Union quickly collapsed. The war had transformed the United States into a world super power with global responsibilities resulting in a continued large federal bureaucracy. American leaders now believed that communism had replaced fascism as the greatest threat to world peace. International tensions and Cold War politics dominated the national news but most Washington residents were more concerned about returning to their prewar lives.

In the years immediately following the end of World War II, the Virginia and Maryland suburbs underwent massive growth as thousands of returning veterans settled in the Washington metropolitan area, attracted by promises of plentiful jobs and low-cost housing. Newly formed private businesses and consulting firms were established in the Washington area to assist the government in its operation while simultaneously offering many employment opportunities to residents of the metropolitan area.

Blacks had achieved significant advancement during the war, benefitting from many wartime jobs opportunities. In 1948, President Truman ordered the complete integration of the United States military, but despite such progress, the nation's capital remained very much a segregated town. A long-time Arlington resident recalled that, even after the war, buses bound for Virginia would stop on the Key Bridge until all black passengers retreated to the rear of the bus. James Lancaster similarly remembered, "Washington was still a very segregated town. There were black theaters . . . there were restaurants in which blacks could not eat. At 14th and Park Road as an example in 1956–57, I was part of a group of people who picketed the Woolworth's 5 and 10 cent store . . . very few blacks lived west of 16th Street which appeared to be the dividing line . . . It was very much a segregated community." The policy of racial segregation in the District was most evident in the city's public school system which openly maintained a two-tiered system of education—one white and one black. Division I schools were exclusively reserved for white students and were universally well funded and well equipped with up to date textbooks, extensive libraries, and modern laboratory facilities. Conversely, the city's black schools, Division II, including Cardoza, Armstrong, Phelps, and Spingarn, were forced to rely upon discarded books and materials from the white schools. Indeed, at Cardoza, lab teachers were often forced to resort to mason jars rather then test tubes for use with science classes.

Because of such obvious inequities, the United States Supreme Court ruled in 1954 that segregation in public education was "inherently unequal," and ordered that the states and the District of Columbia integrate their school systems ". . . with all deliberate speed." While the suburban jurisdictions pledged to resist the court's ruling, the District schools attempted to comply and in the fall of 1954, James Lancaster and 38 other black students were the first to enroll in the previously all white Roosevelt High School. Mr. Lancaster recalled that while the school's classrooms were ostensibly desegregated, the integration of society had yet to be achieved. The school's administration discouraged black and white students from socializing to the extent that such fraternization often led to censure and disciplinary action. One black male student was even involuntarily transferred because of his after-school association with a white girl.

The Civil Rights movement in Washington mirrored that of the nation as District citizens sought the integration of restaurants, movie theaters, and other businesses. In August 1963, Dr. Martin Luther King came to Washington to participate in a march for jobs. Over 200,000 people gathered peacefully at the Lincoln Memorial to listen to the great Civil Rights activist speak. King exalted the crowd, "I have a dream that one day this nation will rise up, live out the true meaning of its creed: 'We hold these truths to be self-evident, that all men are created equal.' I have a dream that one day on the red hills of Georgia sons of former slaves and the sons of former slaveowners will be able to sit down together at the table of brotherhood. I have a dream that one day even the state of Mississippi, a state sweltering with the heat of injustice . . . will be transformed into an oasis of freedom and justice. I have a dream that my four little children will one day live in a nation where they will not be judged by the color of their skin but by the content of their character." In part, because of the demonstration and King's activism, Congress passed several landmark bills over the next few years guaranteeing equal housing, voting rights, and educational opportunities.

On April 4, 1968, Dr. Martin Luther King was assassinated while in Memphis, Tennessee. Shortly after the announcement of his death, violence erupted in the streets of Washington beginning at 14th and U Streets, but gradually spreading to other sectors of the city. Despite repeated appeals by government and Civil Rights leaders for calm, the rioting continued. President Lyndon Johnson finally ordered the United States Army and the District National Guard mobilized to restore order. For the first time in over a century, the nation's government had to be protected from its own citizenry and the spectacle of heavily armed military troops guarding public buildings ap-

peared on virtually every network news program. After several days of scattered violence and looting, order was finally restored but only after 13 people had died and several hundred had been injured.

While anger and frustration among the black community followed the assassination of Dr. King, similar emotions were being experienced by some of the nation's young concerning the continuing involvement of the United States in the Vietnam War. By 1968, the national consensus on the war had been lost and the country became increasingly polarized over the war. Indeed, Jeff Dunson, one of the student protestors, maintained that, ". . . the majority [of protestors] felt alienated from the system . . . because the government did not represent the views of young people." As the seat of government, Washington became the logical focal point for protest against the war.

The scope of the demonstrations dramatically escalated as the Vietnam war continued. In the fall of 1969, over 250,000 people came to Washington to participate in a moratorium against the war. Smaller protests were also common at the Pentagon, the Capitol, and the White House as demonstrators attempted to petition their government to stop the fighting.

While most of the antiwar demonstrations were peaceful, some of the more radical elements in the movement resorted to violence. Several attempts were made to close the government by blocking entrances to federal buildings or disrupting rush-hour traffic. Protestors threw blood on government employees at the Pentagon, hurled rocks and garbage at the police while others engaged in additional forms of street violence. Alan Canfora participated in one such demonstration in Washington in 1969, "Then people started trashing out windows [near Dupont Circle]. I remember the windows of the Riggs National Bank got completely trashed out . . . There was a bit of looting. Police cars got trashed in, too, and a lot of police got hit by objects . . . It was really like guerrilla warfare going on in the streets."

The end of American participation in the war in 1973 followed by the collapse of South Vietnam just two years later, ended the era of protest and discontent in Washington, in time for the nation's 200th anniversary celebrations in 1976. Appropriately, the Bicentennial was commemorated in Washington with the reading of the Declaration of Independence at the National Archives and a splendid display of fireworks. That year the Smithsonian Institution formally opened the Air and Space Museum on the Mall, a symbol of man's quest for knowledge and understanding. In 1982, the Vietnam Memorial was dedicated in tribute to the soldiers and servicemen who served in Southeast Asia. The nation's capital, having survived a decade of strife, turmoil, and disillusionment, now was ready to look forward to a new decade and a new millennium.

Library of Congress

The monument grounds with crowds gathering to hear Dr. Martin Luther King, August 1963.

The Washington Suburbs

The Washington suburbs showed remarkable growth during the years immediately following World War II. Thousands of young, decommissioned soldiers came to the Washington area seeking new jobs, better education, and inexpensive housing. The newly approved G.I. Bill rewarded veterans with low cost housing loans and tuition benefits, making both family homes and college education affordable. In Virginia, the price for a recently built single family home averaged $10,500. With a Veterans Administration approved loan and just $500 down, payments on a 30-year mortgage were merely $65 per month. One author wrote, "The veterans and their wives grabbed for the good things as if there were no tomorrow. They wanted everything at once—home, car, washing machines, children . . . They had babies without worrying about how much it would cost to straighten their teeth or send them to college."

Real estate developers began to acquire large tracts of farmland in the Washington suburbs for new home construction. Edward Carr, for instance, invested huge amounts of money in Springfield, Virginia, for housing developments and shopping centers. Located adjacent to Shirley Highway, homes were advertised as being conveniently located to the Pentagon and the District, just a brief 30-minute drive by car.

The automobile completely revolutionized suburban life. Large shopping centers with a variety of shops and stores were built at major intersections. Even Washington's most prestigious department stores, Hecht's, Woodward and Lothrop, and Lansburgh's, established retail outlets in the suburbs, making the surrounding communities virtually self-sustaining. Many suburban residents ventured into the District only to work or to sightsee when out-of-town guests arrived. Even popular restaurants, such as Hot Shoppes and Top's, were oriented to the automobile. Entire families could enjoy curbside service and feast on such delicacies as french fries with gravy, "Mighty Mo's," and orange freezes without leaving the privacy of their automobiles. Drive-in movie theaters also became popular diversions in the suburbs.

With the post-war baby boom underway, educational opportunities in the suburbs lured many new residents away from the city. In 1950, the University of Virginia established an extension college, George Mason, where college credit classes were taught by university professors in the area's public schools. A formal campus was finally built in Fairfax City in 1965.

The 1954 *Brown vs. Topeka* Supreme Court decision mandating the integration of the nation's public schools, also accelerated suburban growth around Washington. Many whites fled the District rather than send their children to desegregated public schools. In Virginia, Governor Thomas Stanley and Senator Harry Byrd proudly boasted that the state would "massively resist" court-ordered integration.

Fairfax County maintained a segregated school system but there were no black high schools in the county until 1954 when Luther Jackson High School opened in Merrifield. Prior to that time, black students were forced to either attend a regional black high school in Manassas or to enroll in the District. The county's black elementary and intermediate schools were woefully inadequate. None had indoor plumbing or restroom facilities nor were any janitorial services provided, teachers were expected to clean and maintain their own rooms. Bus service was unpredictable or nonexistent, necessitating many students to walk up to six miles to attend classes.

The Commonwealth of Virginia steadfastly refused to integrate its schools. The General Assembly went so far as to suspend compulsory attendance laws for students in integrated jurisdictions and offered liberal tax credits to attend private all white academies. In 1959, the Virginia Supreme Court ruled, ". . . the state must support . . . public free schools in the state as are necessary to

Bethesda-Chevy Chase High School

The intersection of Wisconsin Avenue and East-West Highway. A sign announces the forthcoming construction of a new Hot Shoppe Restaurant. The Washington suburbs showed substantial growth after the war as thousands of former veterans moved to Virginia and Maryland in search of low cost housing and excellent educational opportunities.

an efficient system, including those in which the pupils of both races are compelled to be enrolled and taught." The next year, Fairfax County agreed to admit its first black students. The county school system, however, wasn't completely integrated until 1965.

The Marine Corps Memorial

In January 1945, the end of the war seemed at hand. The Soviet Red Army had captured Warsaw and was advancing on Berlin, the final German offensive at the Bulge had been repulsed, MacArthur had returned to the Philippines, and Franklin Roosevelt had been reelected to a fourth term as President.

President Roosevelt was administered the oath of office on the south portico of the White House. Only 7,806 invited guests witnessed the historic ceremony from the snow-covered south lawn. The President's brief inaugural address urged total victory in the war and called for a durable and lasting peace. The simplicity of the ceremonies, contrasting with the joyous inaugurals of the past, was dismissed as necessary due to wartime austerity programs. In fact, President Roosevelt was severely ill and would live just three more months.

The optimism that began the new year was suddenly shattered in February when an American task force launched a massive assault against Japanese Imperial forces entrenched on the island of Iwo Jima. Three key airfields had been built on the small, volcanic outpost, and the island had been fortified with over 21,000 soldiers, most concealed in hundreds of caves and tunnels. For 36 days, the Imperial Japanese forces under the command of General Tadamichi Kuribayashi waged a defiant cave-and-bunker defense, inflicting a staggering 24,000 casualties on American forces, the highest ever incurred by the United States Marine Corps. Still, the invading American Marines advanced steadily and performed with heroism prompting Fleet Admiral Chester A. Nimitz to report, "Uncommon valor was a common virtue." Likewise, for gallantry on Iwo Jima, the nation awarded an unprecedented 27 Congressional Medals of Honor.

On February 23, four days after the initial landing, six soldiers were dispatched to the 555-foot summit of Mount Suribaci to raise the American flag on the island's highest point. The colors, mounted on a makeshift flag staff, were firmly implanted in the volcanic rock while Associated Press photographer, Joe Rosenthal, recorded the historic ceremony. The photograph of the Iwo Jima flag-raising appeared in hundreds of newspapers and magazines throughout the United States, instantly becoming a national icon and a symbol of the valor of American troops.

Shortly thereafter, sculptor Felix de Weldon lobbied Congress for authorization to build a suitable memorial to the United States Marine Corps in Washington. He received Congressional authorization after the war and over $850,000 in private funds were contributed, mostly from individual Marines.

De Weldon carefully made 36 exact replicas of the proposed memorial, utilizing the three surviving flag-raisers as live models. Finally, after three years of bronze casting in a Brooklyn foundry, the full-scale sculpture was finished. It was transported in pieces for assembly in Arlington, Virginia. Each of the twelve segments was then carefully positioned on the 60-foot concrete base and welded together. The final sculpture stood 32 feet high and weighed over 100 tons. The 10-foot base was covered with black Swedish granite and inscribed with all of the major engagements involving Marine Corps' forces during the nation's history. Likewise, Nimitz's immortal remarks were engraved on the facade of the memorial along with the inscription, "In honor and memory of the men of the United States Marine Corps who have given their lives to their country since November 10th, 1776." Yet the focal point of the monument was clearly the American flag which was authorized by Congress to fly there year round regardless of climatic conditions.

The finished memorial was formally dedicated on November 10, 1954, the 179th anniversary of the founding of the Marine Corps. In attendance were President Dwight D. Eisenhower, photographer Joe Rosenthal, and sculptor Felix de Weldon. The dedicatory address was delivered by Vice President Richard Nixon who stated, "This statue symbolizes the hopes and dreams of American and the real purpose of our foreign and military policy. We realize that to retain freedom for

The construction of the Marine Corps Memorial in Arlington, Virginia. The monument commemorated the historic flag raising on Iwo Jima in February 1945.

ourselves, we must be concerned when people in other parts of the world may lose theirs. There is no greater challenge . . . than to find a way that such sacrifices as this statue represents are not necessary in the future, and to build the kind of a world in which all people can be free, in which nations can be independent, and in which people can live together in peace and friendship."

The six servicemen represented in the monument were Sgt. Michael Strank, Corporal Harlan Block, PFC Frank Sousley, PFC Rene Gagnon, PFC Ira Hayes, and PhM John Bradley. Strank, Block, and Sousley were all killed in subsequent action on Iwo Jima. Strank's remains were returned to the United States and buried at the adjacent Arlington National Cemetery. Likewise, upon their deaths, Ira Hayes and Rene Gagnon were similarly interred at the cemetery. Gagnon's final wish was to be buried as close to the monument as possible and his grave is located just inside the north wall, Section 53 Grave #543. His government stone bears a brass relief of the Mount Suribaci flag-raising and the inscription: "For God and his country he raised our flag in battle and showed a measure of his pride at a place called 'Iwo Jima' where courage never died."

The National Archives

The first wagons from Pennsylvania loaded with government documents arrived in Washington during the hot summer of 1800. The papers were immediately delivered to the appropriate federal agency for storage and future use, but no regulations had yet been developed concerning the proper handling of such materials. The records were often misplaced, lost, or, as in 1814, threatened with outright destruction. When the British invaded the District of Columbia, federal officials desperately tried to save the nation's most precious documents. Stephen Pleasonton, a clerk at the War Department, claimed that he was ordered to ". . . purchase coarse linen, and cause it to be made into bags of convenient size." The Declaration of Independence, together with other important books and journals, were then packed away and carted off unceremoniously to Leesburg, Virginia. Despite such heroic efforts by government workers, many of the country's precious documents were captured and burned by the British, forever lost to history.

Over the next century, little substantive progress was made to improve the efficiency of government recordkeeping. Each federal agency exercised complete autonomy over its documents, frequently with catastrophic results. Treaties, laws, maps, regulations, deeds, and other printed materials were routinely stored in unheated warehouses, moist attics, and humid basements causing widespread deterioration. Presidential papers and collections were also lost after the Chief Executive left office. The voluminous records were frequently inherited by family members who bestowed official documents and letters on friends as memorabilia and often purged the files of any uncomplimentary materials. At Mount Vernon, First Lady Martha Washington openly destroyed the correspondence between her and George Washington while the papers of President John Quincy Adams were sealed by heirs for nearly 100 years. President Harry S Truman later argued, ". . . [the] destruction [of such documents] should never again be permitted . . . [the] truth behind a president's actions can be found only in his official papers and every presidential paper is official."

By the early 1900s, historians were demanding that Congress create a central repository for government documents and records, a facility that would ensure the proper preservation of such important materials while simultaneously making them easily accessible to the American public. It was not until after World War I, however, that adequate funds for a national archives were appropriated by Congress.

Construction on the National Archives building began in 1933. President Herbert Hoover set the cornerstone of the structure on February 20 and remarked, "This temple of our history will appropriately be one of the most beautiful buildings in America, an expression, of the American soul. It will be one of the most durable, an expression of the American character." The fireproof

National Archives

The Declaration of Independence is carefully set into its display case.

Convoys of Army trucks arrive at the National Archives with important documents and records. The Archives is the nation's leading repository of government materials and historic records.

building was finished in just two years but the monumental task of transferring the records of various government agencies took far longer with the outbreak of World War II disrupting such efforts.

The Declaration of Independence and the Constitution were not moved from the Library of Congress to the National Archives until December 13, 1952. At that time, each of the documents' pages were carefully encased and sealed in a helium glass container to prevent further deterioration. They were then escorted by heavily armed guard to an awaiting armored personnel carrier where the documents were carefully laid upon mattresses set upon the floor of the vehicles. When the historic documents finally arrived at the Archives, they were carefully set into a specially prepared bulletproof display case in the rotunda for permanent public exhibit. Each night the Dec-

laration and the Constitution were automatically lowered 22 feet into a special vault located beneath the floor, theoretically capable of withstanding even an atomic explosion.

For most Americans, the National Archives is primarily a place to view the fundamental charters of the American republic. Since its opening, however, the Archives has amassed a truly remarkable collection of federally produced documents, maps, treaties, photographs, sound recordings, and motion pictures. Today, it serves as the central repository for all such government-generated materials. The National Archives proudly boasts that its primary goal is, "Making information available—information on which our Congress and government depends, information for lawyers and the courts, information to educate and instruct the people . . . No longer do these [historical] treasures lie hidden and unused."

The Washington Senators

For 71 years, the Washington Senators baseball team was a vital part of summer in the nation's capital. Despite winning just three American League pennants (1924, 1925, and 1933) and one World Series, the team nevertheless was beloved by area fans. Each season began with renewed hope as the President of the United States threw out the first ball, a tradition initiated by William Howard Taft in 1910. Opening day was a time of excitement in Washington as school children were excused from classes and bureaucrats were secretly absent from work. By mid-May, however, the Senators had usually dispelled the illusions of a winning season and were firmly entrenched in last place.

Griffith Stadium, named for the team's owner, Calvin Griffith, was located at 7th Street and Florida Avenue. It was home to both the Senators and the Redskins until 1961. It was a popular ballpark despite several seats where view of the playing field was partially obstructed by support pillars for the upper deck. Hal Keller, who was the Senator's catcher during the 1949 and 1950 seasons, recalled, "[Griffith Stadium] was a great spectator's park because the stands were close to the

Dwight David Eisenhower Library

Opening Day, 1958, President Dwight David Eisenhower throws out the first ball of the season. The Washington Senators usually finished near last place in the American league, but were still loved by area fans.

field," and remembered it as, "a good hitting park because of the green wall in the center and [its] hard infield."

D.C. Stadium, later renamed RFK Stadium, was built in 1961 after Griffith moved the original team to Minnesota. The city, however, immediately received a new expansion club. Old Griffith Stadium was then slated for demolition because of the expansion of nearby Howard University. The new park was ready in time for the expansion Senators next season but despite its greatly increased attendance capacity and modern facilities, the team continued its predictably poor performance. In 1969, a new team owner, Robert Short, successfully hired Ted Williams to manage the team. Williams, a former Boston Red Sox great who was the last major league player to hit over .400, reluctantly accepted the position, recalling that, ". . . the Senators had the worst organization in the majors, the worst scouting system, the worst minor league talent. They didn't draw, [and] their stadium was in a riot area."

During his first season as manager of the Senators, Williams brought a new sense of enthusiasm and competency to the club. The Senators improved dramatically under his leadership and finished 10 games above .500 for the team's best record in 24 years. Attendance figures doubled despite the highest admission prices in the league and revenues increased correspondingly to the delight of owner, Bob Short. Baseball writers that year voted Williams, Manager of the Year and the franchise's future seemed bright. The Senators' team leader and the most popular player in Washington during this time was first baseman, Frank Howard, who had come to the Senators in a trade with the Los Angeles Dodgers. He was, in Ted Williams' words, ". . . without question . . . the biggest, strongest guy who ever played the game." Known for his powerful home runs, when Howard hit a ball into the stadium's upper deck, the seat was painted white to commemorate the feat.

Despite the team's dramatic improvement and

Old Griffith Stadium, the home of the Washington Senators. The baseball park was popular with city residents until a new facility was built in 1961.

increased fan support, Bob Short personally negotiated a trade in 1971 which brought pitcher Denny McLain to Washington in return for much of the Senators' infield and pitching staff. The trade, consummated over the objections of manager Ted Williams, proved disastrous as the Senators' 1971 season record plummeted. Attendance also declined as few fans were willing to endure exorbitant ticket prices for such inept play. Even such exotic promotions as "free panty hose" night did little to fill the stadium.

Bob Short retaliated against Washington by orchestrating a deal that would relocate the Senators to Arlington, Texas. The move, announced in mid-September, drew an angry response from writer, Shirley Povich, "Seldom has a raped community been offered so wide a choice of villains. The focus centers first on Bob Short, the baseball carpetbagger from Minneapolis who schemed for most of two years to abduct the Washington franchise to Texas."

The Senators still had to complete the season and play a final game against the New York Yankees on September 30. Some 14,460 fans attended the franchise's last game in Washington, many carrying signs and banners denouncing owner Bob Short. After the start of the game, irate ushers admitted an additional 5,000 people free of charge. In the bottom of the sixth inning, Frank Howard hit his final home run in Washington. For several minutes, play was suspended while fans stood and applauded until Howard graciously acknowledged their cheers. Sparked by Howard's home run, the Senators led the Yankees 7 to 5 with two out in the top of the ninth when suddenly, hundreds fans poured onto the playing field determined that the final out in Washington's baseball history not be made. Players and umpires were forced to leave the field and the Senators forfeited the game. They finished the season with a pathetic record of 63-96, $38\frac{1}{2}$ games out of first place. In 1972, spring once again came to the nation's capital but, for the first time this century, no one heard the words, "Play Ball!"

The Kennedy Era

During the early morning hours of January 20, 1961, a heavy eight-inch snowfall blanketed the entire Washington metropolitan area, raising concern about the possible postponement of the inaugural ceremonies scheduled for John F. Kennedy later that day. District work crews and Army personnel from Fort Belvoir, equipped with an arsenal of dump trucks and bulldozers, braved subfreezing temperatures and labored throughout the night . Miraculously, by dawn the city's roads were plowed and passable allowing nearly one million people to line Pennsylvania Avenue to watch the historic festivities.

The optimism and excitement apparent during the inauguration and the early days of the administration were tempered somewhat by Cold War realities, the communist government in Cuba, and the difficult struggle of blacks for civil rights. Still, by November 1963, President Kennedy enjoyed widespread popularity and appeared to be certain of reelection the following year. A domestic political feud, however, had erupted in Texas between Governor John Connally and Senator Ralph Yarborough which threatened to split the Democratic Party in that crucial state. Fearing that

such a division would threaten the party's chances of carrying Texas in the general election, President Kennedy decided to visit the state and personally intervene to heal the political rift. On November 22, after uneventful visits to both Houston and Fort Worth, President Kennedy was tragically shot and killed by an assassin while riding in an open limousine through the streets of Dallas.

No one was prepared for the death of the young Chief Executive. As the stunned nation mourned and grieved, the President's body was returned to Washington aboard *Air Force One*. After arriving at Andrews Air Force Base, the remains were then taken to Bethesda Naval Hospital for an autopsy while administration officials desperately tried to formulate funeral plans. Following much discussion and debate, it was finally agreed to inter the President at Arlington National Cemetery.

The initial plot allotted for Kennedy's grave was just 20 feet by 30 feet and was completely surrounded by a small, white picket fence. An eternal flame was used to mark the exact location of the President's burial. On December 4, 1963, the two deceased Kennedy children were likewise buried beside their father at Arlington.

During the first year following the President's burial, over six million people visited the small grave in what Arlington Cemetery Superintendent Jack Metzler called, ". . . the most tremendous demonstration [of respect in history]." The temporary walkways leading to the grave proved grossly inadequate to accommodate such large crowds. Plans to build a more suitable gravesite were begun early in 1964.

Construction of the memorial grave took almost two years and was not completed until March 1967. On the evening of the 14th after the closing of the cemetery at 5 PM, troops from Fort Myer were quietly deployed around the cemetery to secure the area for the final reinterment of the remains to the new permanent grave. While Robert F. Kennedy, Edward Kennedy, and Robert McNamera looked on, the site was illuminated

John F. Kennedy Library

The reinterment of President John F. Kennedy, March 1967. Senator Robert F. Kennedy somberly looks on as the vault is moved to the new gravesite.

The inaugural ceremonies for President John F. Kennedy, January 20, 1961. Washington was blanketed with a 7-inch snowfall the previous night but city road crews and the United States Army successfully cleared the streets in time for the proceedings.

John F. Kennedy Library

with floodlights. At 6:19 PM, a cemetery backhoe was maneuvered into position to open the original grave. Shortly thereafter, a crane gently removed each of the three burial vaults and lowered them into the open crypts of the new tomb. The entire reinterment process was finished in just over three hours. *The Washington Post* reported, "Without previous announcement, the caskets of the 35th President and his two dead children were raised from their temporary sites last night, carried about 20 feet downhill and reburied . . . [photographs were taken but] will not be released to the public at this time. The prints and negatives are for the family and the National Archives . . . they can be examined at the Archives [only] with

the written consent of the Secretary of the Army."

The permanent John F. Kennedy grave featured an elliptical wall where quotations from his 1961 Inaugural Address were inscribed. The focal point of the site, however, was the eternal flame which symbolized the vision President Kennedy had for the United States and the world. In the words of Melville Grosvenor, the editor of *The National Georgraphic*, "His life was such—the radiance he shed—that if we live to be a hundred, we will remember how he graced this earth and how he left it . . . but the deeds, the words, the examples of the man remain—and there will always be a flame to remind us."

The D.C. Riots

On April 4, 1968, Martin Luther King was in Memphis, Tennessee. While leaving his hotel room, King was fatally shot by a white assassin. In Washington, the first confirmed report of King's death was broadcast at 8:19 PM. Almost immediately, thousands of angry and disillusioned blacks filled the city's streets. Some of the crowds marched through the town demanding that proprietors immediately close their stores in tribute to the slain Civil Rights leader. Incited by rumor and inflammatory speeches, the protest soon degenerated into violence, and by 9:30 the Metropolitan Police were dispatched to 14th and U Streets to investigate reports of scattered incidents of rioting and looting.

President Lyndon Johnson, informed at the White House of King's tragic death, went on national television to appeal for calm, "I ask every citizen to reject the blind violence that has struck Dr. King who lived by nonviolence . . . We can achieve nothing by lawlessness and divisiveness among the American people. It is only by joining together and only by working together that we can continue to move toward equality and fulfillment for all our people." Despite the President's eloquent address, over 125 cities in 28 states reported outbreaks of violence associated with the assassination.

By midnight in Washington, the turmoil had dramatically escalated. Several rioters went on a rampage hurling Molotov cocktails at stores, office buildings, and other businesses. One participant later claimed that the disorders were "a chance to get something you didn't have . . . [it] was something to do. Nobody cared about the next day." Another young girl explained, "Martin Luther King compromised his life away. He had to avoid bloodshed . . . If I'm nonviolent, I'll die. If I'm violent, I'll still die, but I'll take a honky with me."

Police and firefighters were virtually powerless to stop the arson and looting. When they arrived on the scene, hostile mobs angrily attacked the officers and firemen, frequently pelting them with rocks, stones, and debris. By morning, ominous clouds of thick, black smoke blanketed Washington and were visible for miles. President Lyndon Johnson met in emergency session with District officials and Civil Rights leaders in order to formulate an appropriate response to the disorders. The President began by issuing an executive order lowering all U.S. flags to half staff in tribute to Dr. King, the first time in history that such an honor had been bestowed on a black American. Likewise, District Mayor Walter Washington cancelled all events scheduled for the annual Cherry Blossom Festival and the Washington Senators announced that their opening day baseball game with the Minnesota Twins would be postponed ". . . in deference to the memory [of Dr. Martin Luther King]."

The most pressing concern, however, was to contain the rioting and prevent it from spreading to federal offices and buildings. To ensure the safety of government employees, all were released early that afternoon in the hope that the forthcoming weekend would provide ample time to quell the disorders. With all available police personnel already dispatched to the riot corridors, the dismissal of the federal and city workers only exacerbated the situation, clogging all major roads and bridges. *The Washington Post* reported, "The day's violence brought about a serious tie up in telephone service and a paralyzing traffic jam described as perhaps the worst in Washington's history." By 4 PM with the rioting continuing unabated, President Johnson reluctantly authorized the use of the National Guard and regular U.S. Army troops from Fort Myer and Fort Meade to restore order. Over 5,000 troops were quickly deployed to the riot centers. Other soldiers were dispatched to guard the Capitol and the White House, the first time since the American Civil War that federal buildings had to be protected from the nation's own citizens.

The massive military presence coupled with a rigidly enforced 4 PM curfew proved sufficient to stop the rioting. During the turmoil, 13 people

After Dr. Martin Luther King's assassination, civil disorders in Washington and other major cities continued throughout the year.

had died, over 1,000 buildings were damaged, and millions of dollars in property was destroyed. The long-term consequences of the D.C. riots, however, proved even more disastrous. During the ensuing decade, over 118,000 residents fled the city, a loss of 15 percent of the District's population. The destroyed and burnt-out sectors of the city were not immediately rebuilt and for years remained a silent but powerful testimony to a time when the nation's capital burned with rage.

The Vice President's House

The growing urbanization of Washington coupled with the introduction of electric lighting led the United States Navy to move its astronomical observatory from Foggy Bottom to a more remote area of the District. The new site at Massachusetts Avenue and 34th Street was described as ". . . remote from any public road . . . [with the] advantages of seclusion, quiet, and freedom from disturbance." The 72-acre military compound became a center for scientific observation and the nation's leading source of navigational data for shipping. Ultimately employing a staff of over 70 astronomers, the new Naval Observatory maintained seven telescopes, including an antique 12-inch reflecting instrument used in 1877 to discover two moons orbiting the planet Mars.

In 1891, Admiral's House was built on the grounds to serve as the residence for the superintendent of the observatory. The building was later turned over to the Chief of Naval Operations and was the home of such famous naval personages as William Leahy, Harold Stark, Ernest King, and Chester Nimitz.

In 1974, the building became a major source of contention between the Navy and the Congress. Historically, there was no official residence provided by the federal government for the Vice President of the United States. Instead, incumbents of the country's second highest office traditionally lived in their personal Washington area homes which were modified and secured at government expense. After Gerald Ford was appoint-

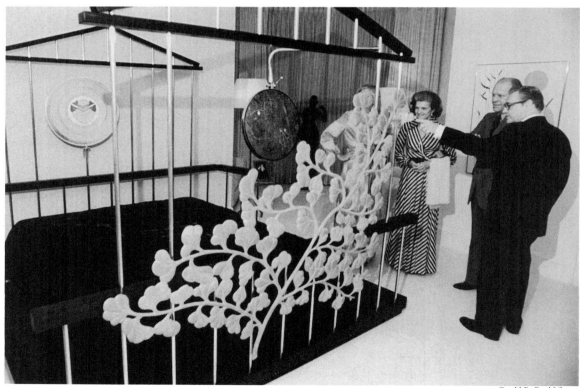

Gerald R. Ford Library

President Gerald Ford listens to Nelson Rockefeller describe a new bed for the Vice President's house. The controversial bed cost over $35,000 and was described as an "apparatus for dreaming." It was removed after Rockefeller left office in 1977.

The Vice President's House at the Naval Observatory. Nelson Rockefeller frequently entertained at the residence but refused to live there.

ed Vice President, his home in Alexandria, Virginia, had to be immediately equipped with bullet proof glass, special alarm systems, and facilities for the Secret Service. Despite the security improvements, protection of the Vice President in such a residence was difficult. Furthermore, with each rotation of office, American taxpayers had to pay for identical security arrangements for the new incumbent, a process many in Congress felt was fiscally irresponsible. Over objections of the Navy, Congress commandeered Admiral's House at the Observatory, designating it as the official residence of the Vice President and approved $500,000 worth of improvements to the structure.

Betty Ford undertook the initial process of decorating the mansion, but events in the Watergate scandal soon propelled her husband into the presidency. Under provisions of the 25th Amendment, Nelson Rockefeller was appointed to complete Ford's term as Vice President and the former New York governor was expected to become the first occupant of the new residence.

Rockefeller, however, was reluctant to occupy Admiral's House. He already owned five houses including a palatial estate on Foxhall Road which he preferred to government-provided housing.

Although Rockefeller agreed to complete the ongoing renovations and to supervise the furnishing of the new Vice President's residence, he steadfastly refused to live there. As a result, Admiral's House was used only for entertaining and other official functions during Rockefeller's brief tenure.

In 1975, the Rockefeller's hosted a series of nine housewarming parties. Hundreds of key government officials, including President Ford, were invited to tour the new official residence. Many, however were stunned by Rockefeller's somewhat eclectic taste and the most discussed feature of the house was a $35,000 bed designed by the artist, Max Ernst. Entitled "Cage Bed with Screen," it was described as an "apparatus for dreaming" and featured a mink coverlet. Although the Rockefellers initially intended to donate the bed after leaving office, the controversy surrounding its design thwarted such plans and the bed was returned to them in 1977.

After Jimmy Carter's election to the presidency in 1976, Vice President Walter Mondale became the first official to actually reside in Admiral's House. George Bush continued the tradition in 1981 and the home is expected to serve all future Vice Presidents.

The Washington Metro

On January 28, 1962, Trolley #766 slowly left the streetcar barn at 8th and M Streets, S.E. A large banner on its side announced the "Last Day of Streetcars!" as Washington's century long tradition in mass transit was about to end, made obsolete by buses, automobiles, and suburban growth. The final route of #766 took the trolley past the Supreme Court and Union Station where hundreds of people waited silently in the cold to watch this artifact of an earlier, prewar Washington pass by. The nostalgic images of the city it evoked, a place of intimate neighborhoods and unhurried pace, had been replaced forever with a large metropolis, the modern capital of a world superpower with global responsibilities.

The dramatic growth of Washington during World War II had likewise been duplicated in the suburbs. After 1945, thousands of news residents and returning veterans continued to move to Virginia and Maryland, lured by local governments with promises of affordable houses, good schools, and low taxes. Areas such as Bethesda, Silver Spring, Arlington, Falls Church, and Fairfax, thrived as federal workers, private lobbyists, and government consultants relocated to the Washington suburbs. Most of these new residents continued to commute into the District of Columbia by private automobile, adding to traffic congestion. Before the war, Washington area traffic jams had been usually confined to the city, but now rush hour extended further into the suburbs, greatly increasing commuting time and the frustration of motorists.

By the late 1950s, it was apparent that Washington's worsening traffic situation needed to be addressed by a comprehensive program devised by local jurisdictions in close cooperation with the federal government. One of the first major proposals called for the construction of a new, circumferential highway to be located 12 miles from the city limits. The expressway, the first of its type in the nation, would completely encircle the

District, permitting interstate travellers to bypass the metropolitan area while reducing local congestion. However, when the Capital Beltway (I-495) was finally completed in 1962, the expressway quickly degenerated into just another commuter artery and spurred yet additional suburban growth as businesses, shopping centers, consulting firms, and housing developments located near the roadway. It became increasingly clear that further efforts had to be made to alleviate the metropolitan area's traffic difficulties.

Proposals for a subway system for the capital had been repeatedly made since the 1930s but budgetary restraints had precluded construction. The Eisenhower administration finally gave its tentative approval for such a facility and created the National Capital Transportation Agency (NCTA) in 1960 to formulate specific recommendations.

The design for the Washington Metro system called for linking the District, Virginia, and Maryland together with 103 miles of track and 87 modern stations. Actual construction on the subway did not begin until December 1969, when tunneling operations were started downtown at the Judiciary Square station. Progress was painfully slow as Metro engineers were confronted with rock, sand, clay, and water. Washington's streets were regularly barricaded or impassable during the construction, increasing traffic congestion and causing monumental delays.

On March 27, 1976, in time for the nation's Bicentennial celebrations, the first portion of the city's subway became operational. Consisting of just 4.6 miles of track and five stations, the system featured ultramodern computerized trains and sophisticated farecard machines. Although initially prone to breakdowns, the problems were soon corrected and Washington's subway became a source of civic pride. By 1986, service had been expanded to include 70 miles of track and 64 stations.

Washington Metropolitan Transit Authority (Paul Myatt)

Construction of the new Washington subway system, November 1973. The Metro opened its first line in 1976, marking an end of over 40 years of bureaucratic arguments and delay.

The Air and Space Museum

The news of the Wright Brothers' successful experiments with a heavier than air flying machine excited Washington residents. In 1908, the United States Army Signal Corps at Fort Myer had expressed particular interest in the invention which was seen as potentially useful in the observation of enemy troops. A reward of $25,000 had been offered to any inventor who could produce a prototype aircraft capable of carrying a minimum of two passengers at 40 miles per hour for at least 60 minutes of sustained flight. Orville Wright was in Washington to claim that prize.

On September 3, hundreds of Washington citizens gathered on the parade ground at Fort Myer to witness Wright's first demonstration of his airplane before a military panel. In the late afternoon,

the Wright biplane slowly took off and flew over the field toward Arlington National Cemetery for 71 seconds to the delight of the spectators. The next day, the Washington papers enthusiastically reported the successful test and, each day, larger crowds gathered at Fort Myer to watch further flights.

On September 17, over 2,000 people were at the parade ground when a young Army lieutenant, Thomas Selfridge, volunteered to be a passenger on one of the test flights. Shortly after takeoff, one of the propellers split and the plane lost control, plummeting to the ground near the western wall of Arlington Cemetery. Wright and Selfridge were pulled from the wreckage and three Army doctors immediately rendered first aid. Wright was seriously injured and hospitalized at Fort Myer while Selfridge was taken to Walter Reed Medical hospital where he died a few hours later, the first casualty of modern aviation. Despite the setback, the nation's infatuation with aviation continued, and in Washington exhibitions of airplanes, dirigibles, blimps, and balloons continued to draw large crowds.

In 1948, the Smithsonian Institution acquired the original Wright Brothers' *Flyer,* the aircraft which had first successfully flown at Kitty Hawk, North Carolina in 1903. The plane immediately became one of the museum's most popular exhibits and the Institution continued to collect other unique and interesting aviation artifacts including Charles Lindbergh's *Spirit of St. Louis.* Finally, the old Arts and Industries building on the Mall was converted into an aviation museum to display such items.

The advent of the space age in the early 1960s likewise captured the nation's imagination. The Smithsonian received several of the original Mercury capsules, including John Glenn's famous *Friendship 7,* which were all placed on exhibit at the Arts and Industries complex. In the court yard, representative booster rockets were also displayed.

It became quickly apparent, however, that the

United States Senate

Senator John Glenn at the Air and Space Museum with his capsule, Friendship 7, *April 17, 1987.*

One of the exhibit rooms of the Air and Space Museum. The museum drew a record one million visitors during its first three weeks of operation.

size and number of the Smithsonian's growing aviation collection demanded a new, modern facility. In 1972, Congress appropriated funds for the construction of a specially built museum to appropriately display such materials. The Air and Space Museum was finally completed and opened to the public on July 1, 1976, in time for the nation's Bicentennial celebrations. It immediately became the city's most popular attraction drawing an incredible one million people during its first three weeks. Besides housing hundreds of airplanes, space capsules, moon rocks, and satellites, the Air and Space Museum was also equipped with a theater, a planetarium, and a research library.

Despite the remarkable design and construction of the Air and Space Museum, some aviation artifacts were still too large to display at the facility. The Smithsonian continued to use the Silver Hill annex in Suitland, Maryland, where restoration and preservation work on aircraft was performed and large hangers were used to house and display larger exhibits such as the *Enola Gay*, the plane which was used to drop the first atomic bomb on Hiroshima. Another museum is planned in the future, tentatively at Dulles Airport for the *Space Shuttle Enterprise* and other aircraft.

The Vietnam Memorial

In 1959, President Dwight Eisenhower, fearing communism's relentless spread through Indo-China, began to expand the American commitment to the fragile government of South Vietnam. Hundreds of United States military advisors were deployed in the region to assist in training the Army of the Republic of Vietnam (ARVN) in its fight against communist insurgents. American soldiers were under strict orders to refrain from engaging enemy forces or participating in combat situations. On July 8, 1959, Army Major Dale Buis was relaxing with a contingent of his ARVN troops at the base mess hall in Bien Hoa located just 20 miles north of Saigon. The soldiers, distracted by a movie, were unaware that several communist guerrillas had successfully breached the base's security. During an intermission when the room lights were turned on, snipers sprayed the mess hall with machine gun and small arms fire, fatally wounding Major Buis and several of his compatriots before fleeing. Buis thus became the first American casualty of the Vietnam War— there were to be 58,131 to follow.

Philip J. Walsh

The statue at the Vietnam Memorial depicting three combat soldiers. It was added in 1984 to honor all American servicemen who fought in the war.

Over the ensuing years, the Vietnam War dramatically escalated, ultimately involving over 2.7 million Americans. During the war's peak in 1968, over 500 American soldiers were dying each week in Vietnam, 16,630 in that year alone. Despite overwhelming advantages in firepower and superior technology, a complete battlefield victory continued to remain elusive. Meanwhile, domestic frustration over the prolonged conflict erupted into massive protests against the war.

In January 1973, some 13 years after Major Buis' tragic death, a peace agreement was finally signed which allowed for a disengagement of American troops in Vietnam. The returning veterans, however, were spurned by an ungrateful nation anxious to forget the painful consequences and lessons of the war. Despite this temporary lapse into historical amnesia, Jan Scruggs, a Vietnam veteran and Purple Heart recipient, was determined that the noble efforts of American servicemen should be formally acknowledged and recognized. He began a remarkable personal lobbying effort for Congressional approval for a Vietnam Memorial. In 1980, a bill finally passed the House and Senate and was quickly signed into law by President Jimmy Carter.

The government authorized a two-acre site for the new monument on land near where the old Main Navy and Munitions complex had once stood. A competition was held to solicit architectural drawings for the memorial. Eventually, 1,421 sketches were submitted for review and the project was finally awarded to a 20-year old Yale University student, Maya Lin. Her plans called for the construction of a 246-foot V-shaped memorial wall of black granite carefully inscribed with the names of all the American servicemen who had died during the war. Lin explained, "Many earlier war memorials were propagandized statements about the victor, the issues, the politics, and not about the people who served and died. I felt a memorial should be honest about the reality of war and be for the people who gave their lives."

Construction of the Vietnam Memorial began

Bill Clarke

Washington's newest monument, the Vietnam Veterans Memorial. Dedicated in 1982. The monument lists the names of all 58,132 Americans who died during the war.

on March 26, 1982, and the entire project was completed in just over eight months. Initially, 57,939 names were inscribed on the wall's 70 panels but after reviewing the cases involving several other military related deaths in adjacent theaters and Veterans' Administration hospitals, an additional 193 names were added bringing the total to its current 58,132. The figure includes eight female Army nurses and 151 Medal of Honor recipients. Each name appears chronologically based upon the date of death. Confirmed deaths are indicated with a diamond inscribed next to the name while those missing in action are marked with a plus. As of 1988, the fate of 2,404 American servicemen remained unknown.

Immediately after the formal dedication of the Vietnam Memorial, friends and family members began to leave small mementos near the names of their loved ones. These included poems, letters, military medals, photographs, MIA bracelets, and other personal items. The National Park Service carefully collects all such memorabilia and chronicles each item for storage at the agency's Museum and Archeological Regional Storage Facility. Other mourners make rubbings of names on the wall as a small remembrance.

In 1984, a statue depicting three combat soldiers was added to the site. It was located, however, some 150 feet away from the actual wall so as not to detract from the monument's central focus, the names of all of those who died in Vietnam. Beginning in 1959 with the name of Major Dale Buis, 16 years are listed on the memorial, culminating in 1975 with Lieutenant Richard Vande Geer, who died during the rescue mission of the *U.S.S. Mayaguez* off the coast of Cambodia. In a city of monuments and memorials, the wall has become one of the most visited sites in Washington, a poignant reminder of those who paid the ultimate sacrifice for the nation.

Bibliography

Bailey, Thomas A. *The American Pageant: A History of the Republic.* Lexington, Massachusetts: D.C. Heath and Company, 1975.

Bigler, Philip. *In Honored Glory: Arlington National Cemetery: The Final Post.* Arlington: Vandamere Press, 1987.

Blum, John Morton. *V Was for Victory: Politics and American Culture during World War II.* New York: Harcourt, Brace, Jovanovich, 1976.

Bowen, Walter S. and Harry Edward Neal. *The United States Secret Service.* Rahway, New Jersey: Quinn and Boden Company, Inc., 1960.

Brinkley, David. *Washington Goes to War.* New York: Alfred Knopf, 1988.

Bureau of the Census. *Number of Inhabitants: District of Columbia.* Washington, D.C.: Government Printing Office, 1981.

Catton, Bruce. "George Washington's Monument." *American Heritage*, December, 1968, pp. 68–72.

Declaration of Independence: The Adventures of a Document. Washington, D.C.: GPO, 1976.

Ewing, Charles. *Yesterday's Washington, D.C..* Seemann's Historic Cities Series No. 24. Miami: E.A. Seemann Publishing, Inc., 1976.

Farnham, F.E. and J. Mundell. *History and Descriptive Guide of the U.S. Navy Yard, Washington, D.C.* Washington, D.C.: Gibson Brothers, Printers and Bookbinders, 1894.

Ferrell, Robert H. *Woodrow Wilson and World War I, 1917-1921.* New York: Harpers and Row Publishers, 1985.

Ford, Gerald. *A Time to Heal: The Autobiography of Gerald R. Ford.* New York: Harper and Row Publishers, 1979.

Freeman, Robert Belmont. "Design Proposals for the Washington National Monument." *Records of the Columbia Historical Society*, 1973-1974, pp. 151–186.

Goode, James. *Capital Losses: A Cultural History of Washington's Destroyed Buildings.* Washington, D.C.: Smithsonian Press, 1979.

Green, Constance. *Washington: Village and Capital.* 2 vols. Princeton: Princeton University Press, 1961.

Gurney, Gene. *The Pentagon.* New York: Crown Publishers, Inc., 1964.

Gutheim, Frederick. *Worthy of the Nation: The History of Planning for the National Capital.* Washington, D.C.: Smithsonian Press, 1977.

Hogan, Bill. "Summer of '42." *Regardie's*, June/July, 1982, pp. 78–88.

Hoopes, Roy. *Americans Remember the Home Front: An Oral Narrative.* New York: Hawthron Books, Inc., 1977.

Horan, James D. *Mathew Brady: Historian with a Camera.* New York: Bonanza Books, 1955.

Howard, Fred. *Wilbur and Orville: A Biography of the Wright Brothers.* New York: Alfred Knopf, 1987.

Johnson, Lyndon B. *The Vantage Point: Perspectives of the Presidency, 1963-1969.* New York: Holt, Rinehart, and Winston, 1971.

Keller, Hal. Letter to Jo Ann Keller. 27 February 1988.

Kytle, Elizabeth. *Home on the Canal.* Washington, D.C.: Seven Locks Press, 1983.

Lakier, Aleksandr Borisovich. *A Russian Looks at America: The Journey of Aleksandr Borisovich Lakier in 1857.* Chicago: University of Chicago Press, 1979.

Lancaster, James. Personal Interview. By Illana Lancaster. May, 1988.

Lee, Richard M. *Mr. Lincoln's City: An Illustrated Guide to the Civil War Sites of Washington.* McLean: EPM Publications, Inc., 1981.

Manchester, William. *The Glory and the Dream: A Narrative History of America 1932-1972.* London: Michael Joseph Ltd., 1975.

McCoy, Donald R. *The National Archives: America's Ministry of Documents, 1934-1968.* Chapel Hill: University of North Carolina Press, 1978.

McCree, A. Letter to Neattie McCree. April 26, 1865. Author's Personal Collection.

Merrill, E.D. "Changing Fashions in Transportation." *Records of the Columbia Historical Society*, Vol. 48-49 (1946-1947), pp. 159-170.

Morrison, William H. *Morrison's Stranger's Guide for Washington City.* Washington, D.C.: William H. Morrison, 1886.

Moulton, Charles H. *Fort Lyon to Harper's Ferry: On the Border of North and South with 'Rambling Jour'.* comp. Lee C. Drickamer and Karen D. Drickamer. Shippensburg, Pennsylvania: White Mane Publishing, Company, Inc., 1987.

Munson, Douglas. "The Process of Making a Civil War Photograph." *Incidents of the War*, Summer, 1987, pp. 7-10.

Netherton, Nan and Ross. *Arlington County in Virginia: A Pictorial History.* Norfolk: Donning Company/Publishers, 1987.

Netherton, Nan and Ross. *Fairfax County in Virginia: A Pictorial History.* Norfolk: Donning Company/Publishers, 1986.

Peck, Taylor. *Round-shot to Rockets: A History of the Washington Navy Yard and U.S. Navy Gun Factory.* Annapolis: U.S. Naval Institute, 1949.

Persico, Joseph E. "The Great Swine Flu Epidemic of 1918." *American Heritage*, June, 1976, pp. 28-31, 80-86.

Rash, Bryson B. *Footnote Washington.* McLean: EPM Publications, Inc., 1981.

Reck, W. Emerson. *A. Lincoln: His Last 24 Hours.* Jefferson, N.C.: McFarland and Co., Inc., Publishers, 1987.

Reed, Robert. *Old Washington, D.C. in Early Photographs: 1846-1932.* New York: Dover Publications, 1980.

Rogner, E.A. *The Pentagon: A National Institution.* Alexandria, Virginia: D'OR Press, Dearengor, Inc., 1984.

Santoyo, Elsa. Personal Interview. July 13, 1987.

Seale, William. *The President's House: A History.* 2 vols. Washington, D.C.: The White House Historical Association, 1986.

Sinclair, A. Leftwich. "History of the Automobile in the District of Columbia." *Records of the Columbia Historical Society*, vol. 48-49 (1946-1947), pp. 143-154.

Smithsonian Institution. Office of Public Affairs. *Yesterday and Today.* Washington, D.C.: Smithsonian Institution, 1986.

Swerdlow, Joel L. "To Heal a Nation." *National Geographic*, May, 1985, pp. 555-573.

Van Dyne, Larry. "The Making of Washington." *The Washingtonian*, November, 1987, pp. 161-320.

Viola, Herman J. *The National Archives of the United States.* New York: Harry N. Abrams, Inc., Publishers, 1986.

Wall, Charles C. *Mount Vernon: A Handbook.* Mount Vernon: Mount Vernon Ladies Association, 1985.

Wartime in Washington. Narr. Daniel Schorr. PBS, 29 June 1988.

Washington: A Turn-of-the-Century Treasury. Ed. Frank Oppel and Tony Meisel. Secaucus: Castle Books, 1987.

Washington Past and Present: A Guide to the Nation's Capital. Washington, D.C.: United States Capitol Historical Society, 1983.

We, the People: the Story of the United States Capitol. Washington, D.C.: United States Capitol Historical Society, 1978.

Weaver, John D. "Bonus March." *American Heritage*, June 1963, pp. 18-23, 92-97.

The White House: An Historic Guide. Washington, D.C.: White House Historical Association, 1977.

Wilson, Frank J. and Beth Day. *Special Agent: A Quarter Century with the Treasury Department and the Secret Service.* New York: Holt Rinehart, and Winston, 1965.

The W.P.A. Guide to Washington, D.C. By the Federal Writers' Project. New York: Pantheon Books, 1983.

Wright, Nina E. *The West Wing: A Brief History.* Preservation Office of Administration, 1984.

Index